RCIA
Team Manual
(revised edition)

*How To Implement
the Rite of Christian Initiation of Adults
in Your Parish*

PATRICIA BARBERNITZ

PAULIST PRESS
New York/Mahwah

Paulist Press gratefully acknowledges the use of a Peanuts cartoon, © 1984 United Feature Syndicate, Inc. reproduced with permission.

Library of Congress
Catalog Card Number: 86:61259

ISBN: 0-8091-2814-4

Published by Paulist Press
997 Macarthur Boulevard
Mahwah, New Jersey 07430

Printed and bound in the
United States of America

Acknowledgements

The RCIA Team Manual comes to publication with debts of gratitude:

To the participants in the National RCIA Training Institutes held over the past four years.

> It was your questions, challenges, enthusiasm and generosity that shaped the spirit of this book. Thank you!

To the catechumens who have shared their journeys with me over the years.

> You taught me what RCIA is, and led me beyond structure to real conversion. Thank you!

To Rev. Kenneth Boyack, C.S.P.

> Your contributions to this work were both supportive and helpful. Thank you!

To Rev. Alvin A. Illig, C.S.P., Director of the Paulist National Catholic Evangelization Association.

> Your idea gave life to the Institute, and to this book.
> Your vision inspired it, and your commitment gave it a chance to come to life. Thank you!

Contents

Chapter V
THE RCIA EXPERIENCE: CATECHUMENATE

Chapter VI
THE RCIA EXPERIENCE: ENLIGHTENMENT/PURIFICATION

Chapter VII
THE RCIA EXPERIENCE: MYSTAGOGIA

Chapter VIII
THE RCIA EXPERIENCE: CELEBRATING THE RITES

Chapter IX
RESOURCES

Introduction

You are about to take on some local leadership in the Rite of Christian Initiation of Adults (RCIA). Congratulations! In addition to hard work, you can expect personal satisfaction, and a challenge to your personal growth in faith. People who have assumed leadership in the RCIA before you will testify that it is well worth the effort.

This manual is intended to help you and your team on your RCIA journey. It is called a *Team Manual*, and we suggest that you use it as a team as you study and implement the RCIA in your parish. If you are beginners, your team may use the manual as preparation for your work. If your parish is already doing RCIA ministry, use the *Team Manual* as part of your evaluation and planning.

Discuss each chapter's topic as a team, and consider what it means for your parish. To prepare for the discussion, each person should read the material in the Manual. Where it would be helpful, use the resources for further study. Always reflect on your own experience in the area of discussion. The worksheets at the end of each chapter can be used to facilitate your parish planning.

Chapters I, II and III call on you to challenge your underlying presumptions about RCIA: *Why do you do what you do?* Chapters IV through VIII help you to look at your parish model in relation to other models: *How do others do what you do?* Chapter IX is there to expand your creative thinking about RCIA ministry: *How can you do what you do better?*

There are three kinds of materials in the manual:

1. *Information and resource leads.* Highlights from basic areas of study and recommendations for further information are included. References listed in the body of the manual include title and author. Complete bibliographical information will be found in the resource chapter.

2. *Samples of sessions, liturgies, role descriptions and interview formats.* The samples should be used as practical examples of how some parishes have implemented the RCIA. They should not be used as they are presented without modification for local parish settings.

3. *Worksheets.* In order to facilitate team use of this manual, questions are suggested for consideration in each parish.

Throughout the manual, we describe a *Composite Model.* This Model is based on the author's experience, which includes working in several parishes in the Archdiocese of Baltimore, as well as diocesan and national offices. The *Composite Model* is described in greater detail than other models to provide a more complete picture to facilitate discussion. While the *Composite Model* is a good one, we do not recommend any one particular model for your parish. A major task for your parish team is to design the model that will work best in your parish community.

St. Augustine Parish in Washington, D.C. allowed us to summarize their RCIA model, and several other parishes have given permission to include a model for a specific period of the RCIA. Because of these contributions, the manual better demonstrates the diversity that exists among good parishes in the implementation of the RCIA. While the written record of the work of these parishes is given just a few pages, the value of their work, and the stories of the people involved could fill this whole volume, and more. We express our sincere gratitude to all these parishes.

Chapter I

Introducing the RCIA

- Overview
- History Highlights
- Conversion
- Interviews
- Who Benefits from the RCIA?
- Parish Worksheet

The purpose of this chapter is to set the foundation for implementing the RCIA, by giving a basic understanding of the process and its components. In the overview, the language and flow of the process are explained. The history section puts our modern experience of RCIA in the context of the past. The pages on conversion show why we do RCIA, and help to focus our attention on the real experience of individuals rather than program components we design.

Interview techniques are addressed, to keep us in touch with what is actually happening for people. And finally, there is a longer section looking at the various groups who may or may not belong in the RCIA process.

The parish worksheet will lead you in discussion of your basic understanding of RCIA, and what it can mean in your parish.

OVERVIEW

The Rite of Christian Initiation of Adults (RCIA) is the process through which adults are fully initiated into the Catholic faith community. It includes four formation periods (evangelization/precatechumenate, catechumenate, enlightenment/purification and mystagogia), and three liturgical stages (rite of acceptance into the order of catechumens, rite of election and initiation).

The first period begins with **Evangelization.** Evangelization as defined in *On Evangelization in the Modern World* means ". . . bringing the Good News into all the strata of humanity, and through its influence transforming humanity from within and making it new . . ." This occurs in both formal and informal ways, but reaches its culmination when a person is moved to respond to that Good News.

That response is welcomed as the first period continues with the **Precatechumenate.** In it, the Catholic Community shares with the inquirer a preview of what it would be like to live out the Good News as a member of the Catholic Church. This first period of the RCIA must be especially flexible in length and in experience, so that the needs of individual inquirers can be perceived and met.

After this period, those who feel that they may be called to the Catholic Community are invited to celebrate the **Rite of Acceptance into the Order of Catechumens.** In this rite, the inquirer requests entrance into the catechumenate and becomes a member-in-training of the Catholic Church.

The second period of the RCIA is the **Catechumenate,** and the person in this period is called a catechumen. During this period, it is the duty of the Church to provide a well-rounded experience of what it means to be an adult Catholic. This must include the four elements of all catechesis in the Church—message, community, service and worship. The central experience of the catechumenate is sharing around the Word, as it is proclaimed in the Sunday Liturgy. **Dismissal** for this sharing usually takes place each Sunday.

The catechumenate period must be long enough for the person to develop a sense of what membership in the Church means. Minor rites (blessings, exorcisms, and giving a Christian name) can be celebrated during the period to encourage the catechumen along the journey.

The period ends with the **Rite of Election** when, on the basis of signs of conversion witnessed by sponsors and other community members, the catechumen is accepted for membership by the community, and makes the final personal decision for membership in the Catholic Church. This rite is the turning point of the whole process of initiation. It usually occurs on the First Sunday of Lent.

This period is shorter in length, and takes place during Lent. In the RCIA, it is called **Enlightenment,** purification, or illumination. It is a time for spiritual preparation for the celebration of Easter and Initiation. The rites celebrated in the community form the center for this period. The most important of these rites are the scrutinies; presentations and preparatory rites are also significant celebrations.

The **Scrutinies** call on the elect and the whole community to scrutinize their lives in light of the gospel message. In the **Presentations,** the Church entrusts to the elect their two most treasured possessions, the Lord's Prayer and the Creed. In **Preparatory Rites,** the Church begins Holy Saturday with ritual anointings and prayers, getting ready for that evening's great events.

The Lenten period ends with the celebration of **Initiation** at the Easter Vigil. The final period of the RCIA is called **Mystagogia.** It is the time for reflection on the mysteries of membership in the Catholic Church. It happens during the fifty days of Easter, when the Church is celebrating its new life and discovering its mission anew every year.

The RCIA experience closes with the feast of Pentecost. It is appropriate to celebrate this culmination by formally recognizing the ministry to which each new member is called.

Overview: RCIA Language
Evangelization
Precatechumenate
    *Rite of Acceptance into the Order of Catechumens
Catechumenate
    Dismissal
    Blessings
    Exorcisms
    *Rite of Election
Enlightenment/Purification
    Scrutinies
    Presentations
    Preparatory Rites
    *Initiation
Mystagogia
(* = Major Rites)

Overview: Period Comparison

"The initiation of catechumens is a gradual process that takes place within the community of the faithful." (#4, RCIA) Acknowledging progress, recognizing changes, ritualizing the steps of the journey, calls for distinctive periods and stages in the RCIA. Each period has its own character. People should know that they have moved from one stage to the next. This comparison sheet suggests how the experience of each period can be highlighted.

Period:	Evangelization/ Precatechumenate	Catechumenate	Enlightenment/ Purification	Mystagogia
Catechetical Method	story telling	catechesis—message, community, service, worship	spiritual recollection	reflection on experiences
Level of Conversion	initial conversion	evidence of conversion	maturing conversion	newly converted
Program Structure	less structured	formal structure	structured, but not catechetical	defined experiences, usually not academic
Connection to Sunday Assembly	informal participation at Mass	Liturgy of the Word/ dismissal	special rites almost weekly	Sunday Eucharist, major event
Name for Participants	inquirers	catechumens	elect	neophytes

4

To understand the foundation of RCIA better, see:

Rite of Christian Initiation of Adults, United States Catholic Conference Publication. The fourteen page introduction in this book gives the guidelines and explanation for these periods and stages. This should be seen as the basic text about RCIA, and should guide whatever is done in parishes.

HISTORY HIGHLIGHTS

In the early days of the Church, the significance of the journey towards full membership was clear, and adult conversion was the rule. The need for an extensive catechumenate, trusted testimony, and a community sponsor was obvious in a Church suffering persecution.

The basic elements of this catechumenate process remained throughout the history of the Church, but its practice was transformed according to the perceived needs of the Church. The following examples illustrate this point:

1. As infant Baptism became the rule in the Church, all the elements of an extended catechumenate were compressed into one rite (the welcome, the signing, the giving of a Christian name, etc.), but they were not eliminated.

2. As time for individual preparation decreased, the time for community preparation became institutionalized. One important factor in the development of the period of Lent in the Church was the need to prepare catechumens and the community for the baptismal celebration.

In recent times, the call for a renewal of the RCIA came from two separate areas in the Church:

1. Missionary lands, particularly Africa, where there was a clear need for a process to guide the conversions that were occurring in great numbers; and

2. Catholic countries, especially France, where the experience was of a population that was Catholic in name only. There was a need to look at what initiation and church membership really mean.

At the Second Vatican Council, the bishops called for a revision of RCIA, and in 1972, the Rite of Christian Initiation of Adults was promulgated. A provisional text was published in English in 1974. With the official English translation of 1988, the RCIA is now mandated for every parish in the U.S.

To understand the history of RCIA better, see:

*A *History of the Catechumenate,* Dujarier.
Presents the story of the first centuries of the catechumenate.

*"An Interview With Balthasar Fischer", *Chicago Catechumenate,* Vol. 6, No. 2.
This interview with the primary author of the RCIA documents sheds light on the discussion and philosophy that underlie the RCIA.

Becoming a Catholic Christian, Reedy.
A series of articles out of the Senaque Symposium on the RCIA, which was effectively the beginning of modern RCIA ministry.

Christening: The Making of a Christian, Searle.
Applies the principles of initiation and Church membership to our sacramental practice. Emphasizes the progressive initiation of children.

Made, Not Born, Murphy Center for Liturgical Research.
A series of articles describing the early implementation of the RCIA.

Also:
"On Sacred Liturgy," #64, 66, *Documents of Vatican II*

"RCIA: An Historical Perspective," Pilla, *Christian Initiation Resources II.* Precatechumenate C.

RCIA, Appendix III: National Statutes and Documentation.

The Shape of Baptism, Kavanaugh.

CONVERSION

The RCIA is a conversion journey. Without conversion, there is no RCIA. To discuss, lead, or be a part of the RCIA, one must understand and be personally open to conversion.

Conversion means change. It calls us to move beyond where we are and where we feel comfortable, to a new place, to a new way of being who we are. Conversion changes the very direction of our lives, where we set our hearts, how we translate our lives into meaning.

Conversion affects every part of our being.

Conversion is *Cognitive;* it gives us a new way of understanding ourselves and the world around us. It brings new images, and gives us something new to think about. Conversion is *Relational.* It changes the relationships we have with ourselves, with the world, with others, with Christ, with the Church. Conversion is *Affective*. We begin to feel differently about things, and to question generally accepted views. Finally, conversion is *Commitment*. When we are converted, we have to do something about it.

Conversion changes the answers we give to these questions: Who are you? Whom are you with? How do you feel about it? What are you going to do about it?

Types of Conversion

Another way to understand the conversion experience is to look at the variety of types of conversion. There is *Affective* conversion, in which one moves from blockage of feelings to acceptance and ability to use feelings. There is *Intellectual* conversion, which moves from viewing knowledge simply as facts to viewing knowledge as the meaning behind facts.

Moral conversion involves the basis for one's choices. It is the move from using law as the criterion for action to using values as the criterion for action. *Religious* conversion deals with one's attitude towards life. Is it a series of problems to be overcome? Or is it a mystery to be discovered?

Theistic conversion deals with one's view of God. Is God a controlling force, or is God a personal being calling for personal relationship? *Christological* conversion involves the move from knowing the Jesus of history to knowing the risen Jesus as Lord, living and active today.

A final type of conversion is *Ecclesial*, our attitude towards the Church. Is the Church an institution, "They", or is it a family, "We"?

Looking at types of conversion can be especially good in helping to view conversion as an on-going process. One is not finished converting, but rather on a conversion journey that does not end. It must affect every aspect of life.

Process of Conversion

Studies agree that there are some common characteristics among people who experience a religious conversion. The first is that they are usually at a time of great tension in their lives, connected with a crisis of some sort. (Marriage, divorce, and moving to a new home are the most common factors.) The second characteristic is that the people have a basic religious world view; they tend to identify themselves as religious persons, who look for solutions to life problems in a religious context.

Situational factors that move such a person to conversion are these: the person is encountered by a member of the religious group at the crisis point ("a facilitating person"), and close affective bonds are formed with several members ("a catching group"). Outside influences are exchanged for more intense interaction within the group ("encapsulation").

Conversion as Grace

In religious experience, conversion is a gift of God, amazing grace. It is the one aspect of RCIA over which we have no control. We must encourage it, accept it, experience it, revel in it, share it. That is precisely what the RCIA process calls us to.

One cannot rush through conversion. The periods and stages of RCIA call each individual and the whole community to acknowledge, accept and progress in conversion.

To understand the conversion experience better, see:

Call to Conversion, Wallace.
Written by the founder of the Sojourners, this book challenges the reader to action.

*Conversion and The Catechumenate, Duggan.
A series of articles highlighting various ways to understand the conversion experience.

Converts, Dropouts, and Returnees, Hoge.
Bishops' study of why people join or leave the Catholic Church. A good sociological presentation.

"Ecclesial Conversion Process: A Liturgical Point of View", Ling, *Christian Initiation Resources II*, Catechumenate C.

"Focusing: A Dynamic Tool for the RCIA", Morgan, *Christian Initiation Resources IV*, Connections G.

Seven Storey Mountain, Merton; and *Turning: Reflections on the Experience of Conversion*, Griffin.
These personal stories of conversion show the consistency of God's action. Without RCIA language, the process is present in each story.

*Stages of Faith, Fowler.
Classic presentation of the process of conversion for adults. Part IV is especially relevant for RCIA ministers.

INTERVIEWS

Interviews play a key role in the RCIA process. The purposes for interviews are: to help each person share his or her conversion experience; to express personal feelings towards the Catholic Church; and to evaluate readiness to move from one period of the RCIA to the next.

Depending on the need, the interview may be with a sponsor, a priest, the catechumenate director, or the spiritual director; it may be one-on-one or it may involve several ministers. Interviews may be formal or informal. Some formal interviews are necessary. Formal should not mean stiff or cold, but it does mean scheduled and purposeful. However, much of the work of interviews will be accomplished through informal contacts: regular contact with sponsors, discussions with catechists, on-going spiritual direction, etc.

Formal interviews should certainly occur before the rite of acceptance into the order of catechumens and before the rite of election. They are also important at the beginning of the precatechumenate, during the enlightenment/purification and during the mystagogia period.

Interviews are meant to be helpful to both the inquirer or catechumen and to the parish community. The spirit must be relaxed and positive. The interview leads to important decisions for both sides, but the interviewer must avoid pushing the inquirer or the catechumen, and must avoid being judgemental.

The interview time provides the opportunity for catechumenate leaders to individualize the RCIA process. The interviewer strives to help the person being interviewed to recognize and to express his or her growth in faith, to acknowledge needs, and to move further along on the journey of faith.

Interviews: *Some Topics for Discussion*
At the Beginning
Background information
Marriage and family situation
Major questions of the inquirer
Experiences of the beginnings of faith for this person

Ask questions like: Tell me about yourself. . . your family . . . Have you ever been part of a Church before? . . . What brings you here?

Before the Rite of Acceptance into the Order of Catechumens
Initial acceptance of Jesus
Signs of willingness to grow
Level of understanding of the Church
The catechumenate and what it involves

Ask questions like: What are your goals for this time in your life? . . . What attracts you to this parish family? . . . Are there any problems or questions you would like to discuss?

Before the Rite of Election
Experience of conversion
Signs of clear change in life
Acceptance of Jesus

Ask questions like: Can you identify some things that have changed in your life over the past months? . . .

What is different about you now? . . . the way you feel? . . . the way you act? . . . your friends?

During Mystagogia
Informed choice of a ministry
On-going connections or roots for the neophyte

Ask questions like: What group have you joined in the parish? . . . What gifts will you share with the parish? . . . How will you be able to minister in your family, neighborhood, workplace?

WHO BENEFITS FROM THE RCIA?

The Whole Church
In a sense, the RCIA is for the whole Church, since it is the process whereby the Church prepares new members for itself. With its dependence on evangelizers, sponsors, and catechumenate team members, it entrusts the task of sharing the faith to each member of the Church. It calls our community to become the holy people of God, who welcomes new members into itself.

To understand better how the whole church is involved in RCIA, see:

Welcoming the New Catholic, Lewinski
A practical handbook for parishes who want to be serious about welcoming new members.

Unbaptized Adults Requesting Membership (Inquirers, Catechumens)
The RCIA is specifically designed for the unbaptized and, as written, makes no mention of other categories of persons. It assumes conversion from godlessness to believing in God, or from believing in false gods to believing in the true God, or from not knowing God to knowing God. It also assumes adulthood, and the responsibility that comes with it.

Others Experiencing Conversion
Both baptized Christians and baptized uncatechized Catholics who want to become active adult Catholics have needs similar to the catechumens, and they are usually experiencing a conversion of similar depth, though it may not be of precisely the same kind. They usually benefit from close connection with the RCIA process, but their special situation should be acknowledged, both catechetically and liturgically.

Baptized Christians
Persons baptized in other Christian churches who wish to join the Catholic community are to be received in accordance with *The Rite of Reception of Baptized Christians into Full Communion With the Catholic*

Church. That Rite reminds us that, in no instance is there to be any confusion between these persons and catechumens. They would normally be called candidates for full communion, and they, the assisting ministers, and the whole parish should be aware of their special situation in relation to the RCIA.

To understand the connection between already baptized persons and the RCIA, see:

*Rite of Reception of Baptized Christians Into Full Communion With the Catholic Church, RCIA; Part II, Chapter 5.

Dunning, "Adapting Liturgies for the Baptized", Part 1 and 2, North American Forum on the Catechumenate Newsletter.
These two articles present a discussion among leaders in catechumenate ministry on the advisability of involving the already baptized in RCIA liturgies.

Duggan, "Ecumenical Sensitivity and the RCIA", *C.I.R.* III, Catechumenate G.

Gross, "Some Ecumenical Dimensions in the RCIA", *C.I.R.* IV, Connections L.

Baptized, Uncatechized Catholics
    Persons who were baptized as infants, but never committed to the faith have a right to Confirmation, Eucharist, and full membership in the community. Part II, Chapter 4 of the RCIA addresses this situation, and basically recommends that we treat them as if they were catechumens.

Practicing Catholics Wanting to Renew Their Faith
    Frequently, active Catholics who get a taste of the conversion and growth in faith experienced by catechumens want to be part of that themselves. Some of these people may be appropriate as sponsors or other helpers in the RCIA process, and they will benefit from the RCIA in that way. In the sense that the RCIA is for the whole Church, it does provide renewal and foster on-going conversion for all persons connected with it, even in a distant way.
    However, the RCIA should not become a general parish adult education program that focuses itself on broad based parish renewal. Any active Catholic who is involved in the process should be there for the purpose of helping the catechumens.
    Active Catholics do need challenge to growth and conversion, and the following movements and programs may be helpful for that purpose:

Charismatic Renewal, National Service Committee, 237 North Michigan, South Bend, IN 46601. (Prayer groups and Life in the Spirit seminars challenge many parishioners to personal and community renewal.)

Cursillo, The National Cursillo Center, P.O. Box 21226, Dallas, TX 75211. (Formal renewal program that focuses on laity, and deepening faith commitment. Their motto is "Make a friend, be a friend, bring a friend to Jesus.")

Genesis 2 and Romans 8, Intermediate Associates, 14621 Titus Street, #101, Van Nuys, CA 94102. (Multi-media adult formation program for parishes.)

Parish Weekend, Hesed Word and Worship Ministries, 8516 Meneola Drive, El Paso, TX 79925. (Spiritual renewal programs for parishes directed by a lay team.)

*Renew, Renew Service Team, Archdiocese of Newark, 1 Summer Avenue, Newark, NJ 07104. Published by Paulist Press, 997 Macarthur Blvd., Mahwah, NJ 07430. (This formal parish renewal program applies many of the principles of RCIA to active Catholics. It is a three year process based on small group faith sharing.) *See also:* Ivory, "RCIA and Renew: Their Relationship", *C.I.R.* IV, Connections B. *See also:* "Renew and RCIA", Caroluzzo, Renew Service Team

Spirituality of the Beatitudes, Justice and Peace Center, 1016 North Ninth Street, Milwaukee, WI 53233. (Adult formation program.)

To Follow His Way, St. Anthony Messenger Press, 1615 Republic Street, Cincinnati, OH 45210. (Six week adult formation program.)

    Parishes that are serious about implementing the RCIA find that they also need good adult education programs, and on-going parish renewal efforts. The RCIA becomes a focus of much of the adult formation efforts in the parish, but it cannot substitute for them.

Returning Catholics
    People returning to active membership in the Catholic Church are experiencing conversion. Because the RCIA is an expression of the reality of conversion, many parishes include returning Catholics along with catechumens. However, in most cases the returning Catholic should be seen as one who has different needs from the catechumen. The experience offered to returning Catholics can be influenced by the RCIA, but it is not the same thing as the RCIA.
    They both need: a chance to tell their story and be heard and accepted; a chance to review and renew their

faith; a chance to hear and respond to Jesus's call in Scripture, prayer, and community; companions on the journey; experience of community; and rituals to mark what is happening. There are differences, however, that indicate that the two groups do not ordinarily belong together. Returning Catholics usually need to re-learn, unlearn, or correct mistaken learnings, while catechumens are learning on a fairly fresh slate; returning Catholics should be focusing on Reconciliation, catechumens are focusing on initiation; and returning Catholics would normally need a shorter period of time for re-entry than catechumens need for initiation.

Parishes with a good RCIA also need a good program for returning Catholics. Program needs are similar—leadership styles are similar—materials, space, liturgical celebrations are similar. There can be some carryover, but the two groups deserve separate attention.

The following are additional resources that may be helpful for the Catholic returning to active membership in the Church:

ANOTHER LOOK: A national ministry of outreach to the inactive Catholic established by the Paulist National Catholic Evangelization Association, 3031 Fourth Street, N.E., Washington, D.C. 20017. Concerned relatives and friends of inactive Catholics are welcome to send the names of these people to the Paulist Evangelization Association. Three times each year, they will write to these inactive Catholics to invite them to take "another look" at the Catholic Church. The request of any person to have his/her name taken off the mailing list will be honored. The names of people sending in the names of inactive Catholics will be kept in confidence.

Experience in several parishes with thousands of inactive Catholics is the basis for *How To Reach Out to Inactive Catholics: A Practical Parish Program*, Rev. William McKee, C.SS.R., Liguori Publications, One Liguori Drive, Liguori, MO 63057.

Catholicism Re-visited is a program developed by the Archdiocese of Louisville to complete an evangelization outreach to inactive Catholics. Written by Alice Hession, it includes ideas for evangelization and for the catechetical followup that should be planned.

Children and Teenagers

Part II, Chapter 1 of the RCIA is entitled "Christian Initiation of Children Who Have Reached Catechetical Age."

Such children are capable of receiving and nurturing a personal faith and of recognizing an obligation in conscience. But they cannot yet be treated as adults because, at this stage of their lives, they are dependent on their parents or guardians and are still strongly influenced by their companions and their social surroundings (#252).

Children and teenagers who request initiation into the community should have the benefit of the RCIA process and the experience of conversion that it fosters. However, it is not always possible or advisable to have them do everything together with adults in the process. Each parish's RCIA team must decide how it can minister appropriately to the young people wanting to join the community.

A guiding factor in this decision making process should be the goal of unity. The decision should not automatically be to have a separate group for teenagers. If people are to become part of the same church, they should be able to be part of the same initiation process. Especially if the young people are part of a family coming to the Church, the best decision may be to make the necessary adjustments to involve several age groups in all aspects of the RCIA.

In all cases, remember that the RCIA does not happen simply in catechetical sessions. There is much more involved. Young people can be part of the RCIA without being present for one or another set of meetings. In addition to the catechetical sessions themselves, look for possibilities for bringing the groups together for social gatherings, liturgies, service projects, etc.

The following suggestions may be helpful in making decisions concerning the inclusion of children and teenagers with adults in the RCIA:

1. In addition to the initiation process, children and teenagers should always be part of an on-going religious education group that is appropriate to their age.

2. If young people are meeting with adults for catechetical sessions or dismissal sharing, consider including opportunities for small discussion groups that will allow for some sharing within age groups as well as the more general sharing among ages.

3. Peer sponsors are a helpful addition, especially when young people are part of an older group.

4. Liturgical celebrations usually are applicable regardless of age.

5. There are many appropriate opportunities for young people to offer service, and that should always be a significant part of their preparation for initiation.

To study the experience of others in making this decision, see:

Lewinski, "A Catechumenate for Youth", *C.I.R.* I, Catechumenate G.

Lewinski, "Towards a Children's Catechumenate", *C.I.R.* III, Catechumenate A.

Catechumenate, Vol. 10, No. 5

Other Groups

Ironically, the very success of the RCIA can become a problem for it. Because it is so good, parishes may begin to see it as a solution to all problems. Parents don't see the reason for participating in their child's religious education? Put them through a modified RCIA. Children aren't regular in attending the CCD? Put them through a modified RCIA. Returning Catholics need an updating in faith? Enroll them in the RCIA. Parishioners aren't volunteering for ministry? Put them through the RCIA. Need a plan for the Confirmation program? Get the RCIA.

There is a danger in this trend toward "borrowing" the RCIA for so many groups. The danger is that the RCIA will be watered down; or, to put it another way, a strong and independent RCIA will never get off the ground. A parish could end up with a hodge-podge.

Once there is a solid RCIA in the parish, however, it will color almost everything else. Sacramental preparation programs for children, for example, have a different emphasis because of the RCIA. Thus, before the Baptism of a child, the parish will look for some faith commitment on the part of the parents, and offer programs to encourage and support that as part of preparation for the child's Baptism. First Eucharist and Confirmation programs will be geared not so much to a certain age but to stages of growth in faith.

Because of the RCIA, which emphasizes adult membership as participating and contributing, the parish's attitude towards volunteers should be different. Members do not volunteer to "help Father", but rather because they feel ownership for the mission of the Church. Adult education programs, too, will reflect the basic notion of RCIA that adult Christians need not only information but ongoing formation as well.

To summarize this point: The parish should allow the RCIA to be itself—the process by which adults are initiated into the Christian community. Once the RCIA is a vital part of the parish, its relationship to and influence on other groups becomes obvious. A parish does things differently because through the RCIA it understands them differently! (*RCIA: What It Is and How It Works*, Barbernitz, p. 38)

This is shown most clearly in the way religious educators are able to use the RCIA as a model in developing programs and materials for use with all age groups. Many good sacrament preparation programs are now designed to use the RCIA as a model; parish adult formation and spiritual renewal programs use the RCIA as a model; and the experiences offered to returning Catholics and others who are experiencing conversion reflect the understanding of conversion found in the RCIA.

Using the RCIA as a model means recognizing that all formation in faith should lead to conversion; that faith is an action of the whole person; that stories are primary vehicles for catechesis; and that formation must include community and service as well as prayer and teaching.

PARISH WORKSHEET

1. How will you help your parish come to understand the RCIA?

2. What kinds of publicity methods will you use to keep the parish informed?

3. How have you experienced conversion? What do you believe about conversion? How can you help encourage it in others?

4. Practice interviewing one another. Encourage personal sharing. Make suggestions about personal interviewing techniques.

5. Inventory the various groups in your parish, and the adult growth opportunities available. What groups do you expect to attract in evangelization efforts? How will you plan for those who need journeys other than RCIA?

6. Who should be part of the leadership for RCIA in your parish? If they are not currently part of your group, invite them to join you.

Chapter II

RCIA: Forming a Church of Adults

■ Adult Characteristics
■ Helping Adults Grow in Faith
■ What Does the Church Say?
■ Implications for Adult Education
■ Parish Worksheet

The purpose of this chapter is to assure that RCIA ministry is viewed with the awareness of what it means to be an adult. One of the most significant aspects of the RCIA is that it tells us that church membership calls for commitment and maturity appropriate to adulthood. For many, this means a switch in focus from children in progressive initiation to adults who are choosing full membership.

This chapter looks at what it means to be an adult, how we can help adults grow in faith, what it means to be an adult church, and finally what implications this has for our education ministry.

ADULT CHARACTERISTICS

The RCIA is for adults. While we recognize a need to study rites ("R"), and carefully pass on the tradition of being Christian ("C"), and look to methods of initiation ("I"), we tend to assume that we all know what it means to be adult. We pass over the "A" in RCIA, and get on with business—but maybe the wrong kind of business.

Understanding adulthood is basic to understanding RCIA. Conversion, church membership, faith are adult actions. For so long, we have made the adjustments necessary to apply the church to children and teenagers that we forget that they are adjustments. The RCIA calls us to remember once again that what we do for people in other life stages we do by exception. The norm is adult membership, adult initiation, adult commitment. We apply that norm and make necessary adjustments for others, but we do not change the norm.

Our recent history had it otherwise. If an adult was unbaptized, we quickly and quietly brought them along to where they "should be" as adults. It was not out of the ordinary to see a celebrant baptizing an adult and using the Rite for Children, addressing parents and asking permission. The RCIA calls us to change, not only our rites but also our understanding of what the rite means.

What does it mean to be an adult? The dictionary tells us that an adult is "a human being after an age (such as 21) specified by law." However, it is clear that more than age is involved in characterizing a person as an adult. As we reflect on our personal experience, we know there is a lack of absolutes in a discussion of adulthood. There are people who are adult in some areas of life, but not in others. Adulthood is not a static state, where one arrives and remains for the rest of life. It is rather a dynamic state in which growth and change will be continuous.

Characteristics normally associated with adulthood include: self-direction; responsibility for personal action; ability to enter into relationships; willingness to make moral decisions; and acceptance of the need to set aside one's personal needs temporarily to help someone else. We see some young persons who may not legally be adult, but who in fact are adult in their actions. We see some older persons who are not adult in action long after they reach the legal age of adulthood.

For a long time, authors wrote about personal development, which had adulthood as its goal. We came to understand childhood and its stages and adolescence and its stages, but all those periods were directed to reaching adulthood. Recently, studies have helped us identify the reality that we do not reach adulthood like the end of a trip, and simply stop journeying. Rather adulthood also

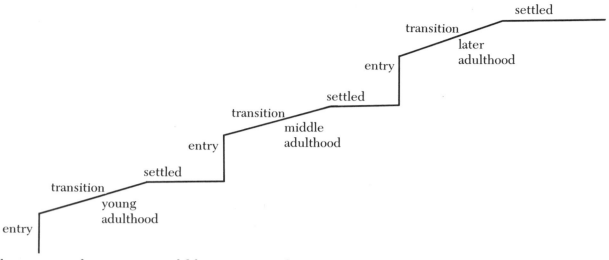

has stages, and a person is on a lifelong journey with recognizable periods, needs, and goals. It helps us both personally and as ministers for others to be able to understand the stages of adulthood, and the characteristics they include.

The stages of adult development are usually divided into young adulthood, middle adulthood and later adulthood with each period further divided into years of entry, years of transition and years of being settled. Consideration of these periods can help us as we plan to do RCIA ministry in a parish. For instance, evangelization efforts can be expected to be most effective for those in a time of transition. People who are experiencing some kind of crisis in their life are most open to the possibility of a change for the better that evangelization offers.

Understanding developmental stages also can help us understand what others are feeling, and how we can be of help to them on their journey.

For a better understanding of the developmental characteristics of adulthood, see:

*Sheehy, *Passages—Predictable Crises of Adult Life*.
The first major work written that addressed the issue of adult development. It is written in non-technical language, and addresses common human feelings.

*Whitehead, *Christian Life Patterns*.
A classic book applying the common experiences of adult change to the work of the educator or religious programmer.

Burghardt, *Seasons That Laugh Or Weep*.
In an autobiographical reflection, Father Burghardt discusses the four seasons of a person's life.

Fowler, *Stages of Faith*.
Dr. Fowler gives examples of the many stages people move through in their faith experiences.

This graph above may help in visualizing the developmental nature of adulthood.

HELPING ADULTS GROW IN FAITH

If adults are developing in other areas of their lives, faith life must also be growing. If it is not, then the life of faith becomes an adjunct to real life, rather than the basic fact of real life. To have faith stop growing at the time of Confirmation, or with graduation from high school or even earlier, almost condemns a person to a life-less faith that has no real meaning for daily living.

James Fowler, Stages in Faith
James Fowler presents the most in-depth discussion of the development of adult faith available today. He identifies six stages of faith that people experience. His research is so helpful because it combines extensive interviews with people at various stages of faith with the development theories of Erikson (psycho-social development), Piaget (cognitive development), and Kohlberg (moral development). His work, together with an extensive bibliography on the subject, can be found in *Stages of Faith*. Because it deals exclusively with adults, and exclusively with faith, it should be seen as a basic text for RCIA ministers. Part IV is a summary section of special relevance.

Specific lessons for the parish team include 1.) accepting each person's starting point in faith as valid and acceptable; 2.) seeing each person's journey as unique; 3.) noting the on-going nature of conversion and growth in faith. We are never finished converting.

John Westerhoff, Will Our Children Have Faith?
John Westerhoff presents another view of faith development that can be helpful for RCIA ministers. His

book is entitled *Will Our Children Have Faith?*, and while it is focused on a child's developing faith, the styles of faith he describes are found in adult believers as well. He emphasizes that each style is a valid style of faith, and is essential to the ones following it.

The first style he calls *Experienced Faith*. The person in this style is primarily imitating and responding to the faith of others. Language used to transmit faith in this style must be accompanied by concrete experiences.

A second style is called *Affiliative Faith*. For the person in this style of faith, belonging to a community is especially important. A sense of authority in the community is desired, and religious affections are especially important.

The third style is called *Searching Faith*. Doubt, critical judgement, and experimentation are part of this style of faith; a strong commitment to a person or a cause is characteristic as well.

The fourth style is *Owned Faith*, the result of real conversion when faith is expressed in deeds and in lifestyle, not just in words.

Probably the most significant aspect of this work for RCIA ministers is the fact that these styles are dependent on one another. So, for instance, we cannot successfully call for the conversion that is characteristic of owned faith from someone whose faith is affiliative. We can do damage to the experienced faith a person has by challenging too much searching faith before affiliative faith has developed.

The image of a tree trunk is used to visualize this theory. Cut across the trunk, the rings of growth show the importance of each stage, and their successive development, and dependence on one another.

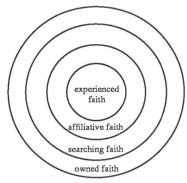

In a parish RCIA group, there will undoubtedly be those in each style of faith. Individualizing the RCIA calls us to pay attention to all four styles, to respect each one, and call forth the growth potential of each one.

WHAT DOES THE CHURCH SAY?

As we reflect on the following official statements from the Church, we should see that we are called to treat adults as adults, and to be a community of adults. Each member is to be respected as a contributing and gifted member. The Church community is composed of members who are members of the political and economic spheres, managers and actors in the world around us. One is not religious in isolation, but rather one is religious precisely in the activities of life. Faith and conversion happen in the real human life of a person, or they do not really happen at all.

Sharing the Light of Faith, National Catechetical Directory, U.S.C.C., 1978.

1. The act of faith is a free response to God's grace; and maximum human freedom only comes with the self-possession and responsibility of adulthood. This is one of the principal reasons for regarding adult catechesis as the chief form of catechesis . . . Rapid changes in society and the church make adult catechesis especially important today. Adults need help in dealing with their problems and communicating their faith to the young. Adult catechesis is also relevant to the church's mission on behalf of justice, mercy, peace, and respect for human life—a mission which depends heavily upon informed and motivated laypeople. Adults need to learn and practice the gospel demands of stewardship: God gives everyone a measure of personal time, talent, and treasure to use for his glory and service of neighbor. Because of its importance and because all other forms of catechesis are oriented to it in some way, the catechesis of adults must have high priority at all levels of the church. #188

Decree on the Apostolate of the Laity, Documents of Vatican II, 1966.

2. For this the church was founded: that by spreading the kingdom of Christ everywhere for the glory of God the Father, she might bring all men to share in Christ's saving redemption; and that through them the whole world might in actual fact be brought into relationship with Him. All activity . . . directed to the attainment of this goal is called the apostolate. #2

3. For by its very nature the Christian vocation is also a vocation to the apostolate. #2

4. The laity derive the right and duty with respect to the apostolate from their union with Christ their head . . . They are assigned to the apostolate by the Lord himself. #3

5. From the reception of these charisms or gifts, including those which are less dramatic, there arise for each believer the right and duty to use them in the

church and in the world for the good of mankind and for the upbuilding of the church. In so doing, believers need to enjoy the freedom of the Holy Spirit who breathes where he wills. #3

6. Promoting Christian friendship among themselves, they help one another in any kind of necessity. #4

7. The church shows herself to be wholly united around Christ by the bond of charity. So too, in every era she is recognized by this sign of love, and while she rejoices in the undertakings of others, she claims works of charity as her own inalienable duty and right. For this reason, pity for the needy and the sick, and works of charity and mutual aid intended to relieve human needs of every kind are held in special honor by the church. #8

8. The apostolate of the social milieu, that is, the effort to infuse a Christian spirit into the mentality, customs, laws, and structures of the community in which a person lives, is so much the duty and responsibility of the laity that it can never be properly performed by others. In this area the laity can exercise the apostolate of like toward like. It is here that laymen add to the testimony of life the testimony of their speech; it is here in the arena of their labor, profession, studies, residence, leisure, and companionship that laymen have a special opportunity to help their brother. #13

9. Above all, however, the lay person should learn to advance the mission of Christ and the Church by basing his life on belief in the divine mystery of creation and redemption, and by being sensitive to the movement of the Holy Spirit, who gives life to the people of God and who would impel all men to love God the Father as well as the world and mankind in him. This formation should be deemed the basis and condition for every successful apostolate. #29

10. This most sacred Council, then, earnestly entreats in the Lord that all laymen give a glad, generous, and prompt response to the voice of Christ, who is giving them an especially urgent invitation at this moment. (#33)

Dogmatic Constitution on the Church, Chap. IV, The Laity. Documents of Vatican II, 1966.

11. The laity are in their own way made sharers in the priestly, prophetic, and kingly functions of Christ. They carry out their own part in the mission of the whole Christian people with respect to the Church and the world.

12. The laity, by their very vocation, seek the kingdom of God by engaging in temporal affairs and by ordering them according to the plan of God. #31

13. Upon all the laity, therefore, rests the noble duty of working to extend the divine plan of salvation ever increasingly to all men of each epoch and in every land. Consequently, let every opportunity be given them so that, according to their abilities and the needs of the times, they may zealously participate in the saving work of the Church. #33

14. During the celebration of the Eucharist, these daily actions and sacrifices are most lovingly offered to the Father along with the Lord's body. Thus as worshipers whose every deed is holy, the laity consecrate the world itself to God. #34

15. Each individual layman must stand before the world as a witness to the resurrection and life of the Lord Jesus and as a sign that God lives. #38

Called and Gifted: The American Catholic Laity (Reflections of the American Bishops Commemorating the Fifteenth Anniversary of the Issuance of the Decree on the Apostolate of the Laity)

16. The adult character of the People of God flows from baptism and confirmation which are the foundation of the Christian life and ministry. They signify initiation into a community of believers who, according to their state of life, respond to God's call to holiness and accept responsibility for the ministry of the Church.

17. Baptism and confirmation empower all believers to share in some form of ministry.

18. Christian service or ministry broadly understood includes civic and public activity, response to the imperatives of peace and justice, and resolution of social, political, and economic conflicts, especially as they influence the poor, oppressed and minorities.

19. Just as by divine institution bishops, priests, and deacons have been given through ordination authority to exercise leadership as servants of God's people, so through baptism and confirmation lay men and women have been given rights and responsibilities to participate in the mission of the Church.

20. The Christian faithful . . . are called to exercise the mission which God has entrusted to the Church to fulfill in the world, in accord with the condition of each one. (204)

21. All the Christian faithful must make an effort, in accord with their own condition, to live a holy life and to promote the growth of the Church and its continual sanctification. (210)

22. The Christian faithful are free to make known their needs . . . to the pastors of the Church . . . ; they have the right and even at times a duty to manifest to the sacred pastors their opinion on matters which pertain to the good of the Church. (212)

23. All the Christian faithful, since they participate in the mission of the Church, have the right to promote or to sustain apostolic action by their own undertakings in accord with each one's state and condition; however, no undertaking shall assume the name Catholic unless the consent of competent ecclesiastical authority is given. (216)

24. They enjoy a lawful freedom of inquiry, and the right to prudently express their opinions on matters in which they have expertise, while observing a due respect for the magisterium of the Church. (218)

25. The laity . . . are bound by the general obligations and enjoy the general right to work as individuals or in associations so that the divine message of salvation becomes known and accepted by all persons throughout the world. (225)

26. Lay persons who excel in the necessary knowledge, prudence, and uprightness are capable of assisting the pastors of the Church as experts or advisors; they can do so even in councils, in accord with the norm of law. (228)

27. Lay persons who devote themselves . . . to some special service of the Church are obliged to acquire the appropriate formation which is required to fulfill their function properly and to carry it out conscientiously, zealously, and diligently. (231)

IMPLICATIONS FOR ADULT EDUCATION

We are challenged to understand the RCIA in terms of our understanding of adulthood. Our Church is an adult Church. Worship is an adult action. Faith is an adult response. Our education methodology must be adult.

James DeBoy, in his book, *Getting Started in Adult Religious Education*, distinguishes between adult learning, adult education, and schooling. Adult learning is happening all the time, through ordinary communication and events of daily life. Schooling refers to a structured plan for comprehensive learning, and attitudes towards that term usually are colored by experience of school as a child. Adult education includes elements of both, and can be described as the intentional effort to provide learning opportunities for adults.

There is general agreement that education methods for adults, and probably for younger people as well, should include certain elements: recognition of life experience and current knowledge; identification of personal learning goals; opportunity for active participation in the learning process; application to daily life; and effective presentation of new material.

One of the major elements of RCIA ministry in the parish is finding the person best qualified to be the primary catechist. It should be the very best adult educator in the parish. This is not always the best theologian; not always the professional teacher. Skills of the adult catechist include group facilitation, knowledge of resources, and a willingness to share personal faith.

It is essential that the RCIA Team insure that adult methodology be used throughout the RCIA process. If the dual gifts of facilitation and theological expertise do not belong to the same person, a partnership should be forged. Consider having one person do a presentation, followed by a second person leading a process of incorporation. (In one parish, a laywoman described her role like this: "Father teaches for about one half hour each evening, and then I tell them what he said.")

Thomas Groome's critical praxis method is an excellent example of such educational principles. In brief, the method involves these five movements:

1. Present action: the participants are invited to name their own activity concerning the topic for attention.

2. Critical reflection: they are invited to reflect on why they do what they do, and what the likely or intended consequences of their action are.

3. Story and its vision: the educator makes present to the group the Christian community's story concerning the topic at hand and the faith response it invites.

4. Dialectic between Story and stories: the participants are invited to appropriate the Story to their lives in a dialectic with their own stories.

5. Dialectic between Vision and visions: there is an opportunity to choose a personal faith response for the future.

(Groome, Thomas, *Christian Religious Education*, Harper & Row, New York, 1980, Chapters 9 and 10)

Understanding the Right and Left
Hemispheres of the Brain

One of the most valuable new insights into educational methodology has come from the observations of neurologists and brain surgeons. Their studies show the connections between various kinds of human activity and the physical makeup of the brain. It has led educators of all kinds to see the need to communicate with the total person, with both the right and left sides of the brain.

The brain has two very separate hemispheres or lobes. The left lobe controls the right side of the body, and is the place where language, speech, verbal memory, mathematics, and a sense of time happen. The right lobe of the brain controls the left side of the body, and it is non-verbal, holistic, synthetic, intuitive, and timeless.

When we work to prepare new members for the church, we must have concern for both sides of the brain. Concern in the catechumenate for doctrine, and specific practices reach the left side of the brain. Concern for developing self-identity as a Catholic, for feeling membership in the community, for developing instincts and intuitions of a Catholic reach the right side of the brain. The whole brain gets baptized!

Understanding this phenomenon of right/left brain can also help us appreciate the individual styles of learning, of leadership, and of membership.

People who are used to using only left brain (which has traditionally been seen as the way to *really* learn) will want a catechism with clear questions and answers, and a calendar with an absolute schedule of events. A team that is concerned with the total person will help each learner develop right side activities as well, through personal sharing, art, literature, discussion, and centering prayer.

Without modern language the Catholic tradition has always communicated with both right and left lobes of the brain. Consider these examples from our Catholic tradition:

Our buildings that impel us towards God without words;

Our well-developed symbol language that calls each believer to appreciate water, bread, wine, oil, touch in a way that the left brain never could;

Our tradition of prayer that is both verbal and non-verbal, centering prayer, contemplation and meditation.

All express and encourage right and left lobe communication with our God.

Religious educators are moving out of a generation that concentrated on left lobe learning—doctrine, numbers, and structures. Without abandoning this valid part of our Church, we must always also encourage right lobe learning—integrating, personalizing, symbol-making, faith-ing.

In our sessions, on our teams, in the membership styles we encourage, both left and right brain gifts are needed.

Storytelling as a Catechetical Method

When we apply the best of educational theories to adults and their needs, the catechetical method that results is storytelling. Each inquirer or catechumen has a valuable story; each sponsor, catechist, leader has a valuable story; Jesus, the Church, Scripture give us our Master Story, unifying us with our tradition. Particularly in the RCIA, storytelling is the appropriate methodology.

In evangelization, it is the story of Jesus that is ultimately shared: "We seek to convert solely through the power of the message proclaimed." (Evangelii Nuntiandi, #18)

In precatechumenate, the story of each inquirer is the content for the faith discussion that occurs. Leadership involves helping each person come to understand and appreciate his or her own personal story. Each needs the time, the skills and the freedom to be able to verbalize it. On our part, the responsibility is to listen to each story, show absolute respect for it, and encourage acceptance of each individual by the whole community. Another side of precatechumenate ministry is sharing the essence of the Church's story. We enter into dialogue with our stories both by listening and speaking.

The catechumenate period is the time for telling the story of Jesus and the story of the Church. It is to be organized and presented in an understandable fashion. The story is clearest when it is read in the life experience of a good Catholic community, and its members. To understand the curriculum of the catechumenate as story implies that it is a personal faith story. Teaching in the catechumenate means sharing the real lived faith of a community of people, not teaching chapters 1 to 25 of a catechism.

In the Enlightenment period, our story is laid bare before God, ready for the impact God will have on it. Our story becomes the story of the Spirit; and we become new.

And finally, in mystagogia, the neophyte becomes part of the story of the Church, and the experience of Church becomes different for all of us.

To speak of storytelling as a catechetical method

does not mean flighty exercises in fantasy. Rather it means revealing what is within. Story is personal; story is of the essence of truth; story is what makes me what I am and what makes us what we are.

Teaching content apart from personal commitment is informational, and may satisfy the mind, but it is not the business of RCIA. Storytelling makes the content personal in its source, and personal in its goal. That is the business of RCIA.

To learn more about methods for adult learning, see:

DeBoy, *Getting Started in Adult Religious Education.*
This book describes methods and planning ideas for good parish based adult formation.

Knowles, *The Modern Practice of Adult Education: Andragogy Versus Pedagogy.*
This is the classic study for adult education, used in most study programs preparing adult educators.

Also:
Hughs, *Ministering to Adult Learners: A Skills Workbook for Christian Education Leaders.*

Parent, *Christian Adulthood: A Catechetical Resource 1982; 1983; 1984.*

Schaefer, *Program Planning for Adult Christian Education.*

PARISH WORKSHEET
1. In your parish, what experiences do adults have that confirm their adulthood, and call them to respond as adults?

2. What experiences do adults have in your parish that treat them as less than adult?

3. Test out the idea of developmental stages of adulthood in your own life. Does it make sense from your experience? Share your feelings about this with one another.

4. Who in your parish has the skills for adult catechesis?

5. How can you develop skills for adult learning in others?

6. Reflect on your own faith story, and begin to share it with someone else.

Chapter III

The Parish RCIA Team

- Team Concept
- Specific Team Roles
- Parish Community as Minister
- Interviews With Team Members
- Team Tasks
- Parish Worksheet

The purpose of this chapter is to discuss leadership needs for local implementation of the RCIA. "None of us is as smart as all of us." It is essential that local leadership be team leadership.

The chapter describes the various tasks involved in RCIA ministry and suggests some of the ways teams might structure themselves to accomplish these tasks. Methods for involving the whole parish are suggested.

The interviews with team members represent a variety of parish settings. They highlight both the diversity and the similarity among parishes as they work to initiate new members. And finally, some of the major programming tasks of the team are listed for consideration.

TEAM CONCEPT

A key step as a parish begins to implement the RCIA is finding and developing appropriate local leadership. This is one of the many significant differences between old style instruction and the RCIA. The former had one leader. That one person was usually the priest. He was well-trained, resourceful, interested, and usually compassionate and helpful. The RCIA is different in that it requires shared leadership among many people. Regardless of how well-trained or competent, no matter how much time the person has available, one person cannot "do the RCIA."

#9 of the Introduction to the RCIA says, ". . . the people of God, as represented by the local church, should understand and show by their concern that the initiation of adults is the responsibility of all the baptized." The team should see its role as enabling the whole community, and representing it to the catechumens.

Team membership should be at least somewhat representative of the community. It should include lay, religious, and clergy. Efforts should be made to involve people from a variety of age groups, races, geographical areas, and religious styles. Teams should regularly judge themselves on the basis of such diversity. If ever the RCIA is seen as "belonging" to one or another segment of the parish, it will be limited in its effectiveness.

Developing Your Team

When a parish decides to implement the RCIA, one of the first steps should be gathering a leadership team. Some people would automatically become part of that team: the person who knows the inquirers best (often the one who had been doing most of the instructions previously); the person who discovered RCIA and brought enthusiasm for it to the local parish.

Look beyond those natural members to other possibilities: a new member of the church with two or three years experience; a representative of the "old guard" in your parish, who would be happy that the church is still trying to get new members; representatives from one or two related structures in your parish, like the committee for education, liturgy, or evangelization.

That usually small beginning team should study the RCIA process and talk with people from other parishes who have experienced it. Then, even before they feel ready, they should begin—jump into the RCIA waters, and start the on-going process of learning, growing, and doing all at the same time.

Most beginning teams have only three or four members; as the process develops, the need for specific additional people becomes clear, and others are added to the team to meet those needs.

As the parish becomes experienced in the RCIA, the team becomes more organized. Usually it also becomes larger. Depending on the size of the parish, workable teams range in size from three people to as many as twelve people. Some parishes design a structure that includes committees of the basic team, so that more people are exercising specific roles. Whatever structure develops, remember to evaluate it regularly on the basis of the needs of the catechumens, and the spirit of the RCIA.

Some cautions: Don't forget that the team needs ongoing care, and that the process should be helpful for them as well as for the catechumens; *but* remember that the process is for the catechumens. Team members and their needs are not to overwhelm those of the catechumens.

Don't get cemented into one structure. Question the way you are organized frequently to see if it is as productive as it can be; *but* don't spend your team time navel gazing, and concentrating on yourselves.

Don't be afraid of new blood; don't become so comfortable that you get into a rut; don't change just for the sake of changing; *but,* do change. It's the only way to grow and improve. So, do plan for turnover, and for including new people.

For more information about the necessity for team leadership in the RCIA, see:

Boyack, *A Parish Guide to Adult Initiation.* (This book describes team roles in detail, and suggests how a parish could prepare for the first year's experience of RCIA.)

Brodeur, "Ministries in the RCIA", *C.I.R.*, I, Catechumenate D.

McEvoy, "Who Are the Ministers of the RCIA?", *C.I.R.*, III, Catechumenate B.

Vertreace, Martha M., "Lay Ministries for the RCIA", *Chicago Catechumenate*, Vol. 4, No. 3.

SPECIFIC TEAM ROLES

Note: These titles refer to roles or tasks that are present in every parish implementing the RCIA. Depending on local circumstances, one person with one title may assume several roles. The titles are not important; the tasks are.

RCIA Coordinator

This person is responsible for coordinating the parish team and its efforts at parish implementation of the RCIA, under the direction of the pastor, and in concert with the total parish community. It is his/her special responsibility to be aware of the overall process and how the parts fit together.

Primary Catechist

With the direction of the team, this person is responsible for the catechesis in the RCIA; special attention is to be given to the quality, completeness, and appropriateness of the catechesis. Often this person will be working with several other catechists for actual sessions.

Evangelizer

In most cases, this person will be a representative of the parish Evangelization Committee. He/she has special responsibility to assure planned evangelization efforts directed to participation in the precatechumenate and catechumenate in the parish. During mystagogia this team member helps to maximize the neophyte's charism for evangelization.

Sponsor Coordinator

In consultation with the team, the Sponsor Coordinator is responsible for recruiting, training and assigning sponsors, as well as the follow-up support for the sponsors in the parish.

Sponsor

While sponsors are not members of the parish team, their contribution to the process is key. It is they who individualize the RCIA, and they are often the best judge of the shape of the journey for the people in it. As the parish appoints sponsors, they fulfill an important part of their responsibility in the process of initiation.

To learn more about the role of sponsor, see:

Dowd, "Witness and Guide: Role of Sponsor in the RCIA", *C.I.R.* I, Catechumenate F.

Naegel, "Sponsoring: A Case Study", *C.I.R.* III, Catechumenate J.

Lewinski, *A Guide for Sponsors*
This book is appropriate to give to potential sponsors to help them grasp the spirit of the ministry they are asked to accept.

Pastor

If the pastor is not part of the parish team by virtue of another specific role, his participation is still needed on the team as pastor. While it may not be necessary for him to be present for every meeting, successful implementation of the RCIA requires the pastor's support and encouragement, his personal commitment to the process, and an openness to the parish wide implications of the RCIA.

Spiritual Director

This team member focuses attention on both individual and group spiritual growth. Responsibilities include the overall prayer life of the catechumenal community: providing a variety of prayer experiences; developing the special character of the enlightenment/purification period; and individual spiritual direction (or pastoral counseling, or spiritual friendship) for the catechumens, helping them build the foundation for an on-going plan of spiritual direction. This role may be filled by one person, or, like the role of sponsor coordinator, may mean recruiting and training several parishioners to offer on-going personal spiritual direction.

To learn more about the role of spiritual director, see:

Carroll, "Spiritual Direction and the Neophyte", *C.I.R.* IV, Mystagogia A.

*Dyckman and Carroll, *Inviting the Mystic, Supporting the Prophet*.
This book identifies the gifts for spiritual direction that can be found in non-professionals. It assumes the fact that God gifts the community with the gifts it needs.

Gula, "Spiritual Direction in the RCIA", *C.I.R.* IV, Precatechumenate D.

Irving and Campbell, "Spiritual Direction and the RCIA: A Matter of Relationship", *C.I.R.* IV, Catechumenate B.

Liturgy Planner

This team member must work closely with the other parish liturgical structures—liturgy committee, music ministers, clergy—to prepare for and coordinate the celebrations of rites for the RCIA. He/she insures that the parish, the catechumens, and the celebrants are prepared for their appropriate roles.

Other Team Roles Identified in Parishes:
    Parish Contact Person
    Hospitality Coordinator
    Follow-up Activities Coordinator
    Precatechumenate Coordinator
    Catechumenate Coordinator
    Enlightenment Coordinator
    Mystagogia Coordinator

To learn more about the development of a team, see:

Boyack, *A Parish Guide To Adult Initiation*.
This book describes how a parish can begin RCIA ministry through developing a representative team from among the parish.

Dunning, *New Wine, New Wineskins*.
This presentation about the RCIA highlights the importance of team ministry throughout.

PARISH COMMUNITY AS MINISTER

Once we master the challenge of making RCIA leadership team leadership, we receive still a further challenge: ". . . the initiation of adults . . . is the business of *all* the baptized." (#41, RCIA)

In the RCIA, the parish community is the primary minister of initiation. When you ask a catechumen "Who is initiating you?" the answer should be "the parish." It is this challenge from the RCIA that leads to its being listed as a parish renewal program. (We should not see it primarily as a parish renewal program, but if we are serious about enabling the parish to have a hand in initiating, we are renewing the parish.)

Probably this is the aspect of the RCIA that we are furthest from achieving, but that doesn't mean we should stop trying, but rather that we should try all the harder.

There are two aspects of this challenge: one that the parish be perceived as the initiating agent. Catechumens should really feel welcome by the parish. In a sense, that is what initiation is all about. Apart from RCIA talk, the only place we use the word initiation is when we talk about clubs, or fraternities—initiation brings to mind some weird kinds of things that people do to others. But, while Christian initiation will never be weird or scary, it should be initiation.

Initiation is what the group does to you when you want to be a member. The group acts on you, and when they are finished, you are a member, a part of the "in" group. You do not become a member by learning about the history of the group. You do not become a member because someone tells you you are a member. You become a member when you are accepted as a member by the group. And that is what initiation is all about.

The other side of the issue is that the parish really is doing the initiating. Teams must insure that there are ways for the parish to truly be a part of the initiating activity. True, most of the work is done by the team, but the parish should know what is happening, feel a part of it, and have at least a minimum way of being part of it. Some ideas about how to help this happen in a parish are:

1. Provide opportunities for parishioners to offer expressions of welcome at liturgies and other parish func-

tions. Have the catechumens standing at the door of the church; have special seats for them, and identify them clearly as people joining the church.

2. Encourage contact with catechumens outside of parish facilities. If their faces and names become familiar enough, parishioners will recognize them in neighborhood stores, on the street, or elsewhere. Remind parishioners to speak to them, and recognize them as catechumens.

3. Publish names of catechumens. Make addresses and phone numbers available to interested responsible parishioners. A note or phone call to introduce yourself, say welcome, promise prayer, and perhaps offer a ride or a visit can be a practical action for many parishioners.

4. Request that the parish council and parish committees and organizations take responsibility for finding a way to make themselves known to catechumens. Consider scheduling a different organization for each week's session; one or more representatives from that group would open the session with a short presentation about their ministry in the parish, and how the new member might be part of that service. The visitors would then take part in the discussion of the evening's sessions, and stay afterwards for discussion, and refreshments which they provide.

5. Provide for active participation of parishioners in the rites and the formation sessions. Include as many people as possible. Parish council members can do the presentations; neighbors and family members can give a special blessing; people from the congregation can sign with the sign of the cross.

6. Give specific tasks to people in specific ministries:
Ushers should recognize catechumens, and know where they sit, and what they are doing;
Lectors can mention the catechumens in their greetings or introductory words;
Leaders of the prayer of the faithful can include the catechumens in the intentions;
Parishioners who distribute food to the needy, or visit hospitals, should know if they are dealing with a catechumen, and know how to invite someone to become a catechumen.

7. Consider assigning shut-ins in the parish as "prayer partners" for catechumens. One of the activities catechumens could be asked to do is to visit shut-ins in the parish during their time of preparation for the purpose of sharing faith with them. The shut-in has a

unique experience of church and its value, even when physical presence is not possible. And the prayer of the shut-in person has a special power, and is a beautiful sign of the mystical body of Christ.

8. Take every opportunity to develop ministries beyond the RCIA team. Make the primary catechist a coordinator of catechists; the spiritual director a coordinator of spiritual friends; and the coordinator of sponsors a true coordinator of many. Resist the temptation to allow sponsors and other ministers to automatically repeat their ministry year after year; force your team to find new people, expanding the number of parishioners who have been directly connected to the RCIA.

To read more about the importance of the parish in RCIA ministry, see:

Barbernitz, "Setting Some Standards for RCIA", *C.I.R.* IV, Catechumenate G.

Ling, "The Catechumenate: The Community as Catechist", *C.I.R.* I, Catechumenate B.

INTERVIEWS WITH TEAM MEMBERS

Catechumenate Director
John Butler, Saint Augustine Parish
Washington, D.C.

1. *How is your parish organized for the RCIA? Describe your catechumenate team.*

We have a catechumenate director, who is responsible for the overall direction of the process in the parish. Our pastoral team includes two priests, and they rotate year to year as chief catechist, and that catechist is on the team.

There is also a coordinator for sponsors, who sat through the process once as a participant looking for renewal and personal updating; a second time as a sponsor; and now she serves as coordinator for sponsors.

We have a minister of hospitality, and finally, there is a spiritual director. At this point, this role is filled by the parish priest who is also chief catechist.

2. *Describe your responsibilities as catechumenate director.*

A major function of the director is to facilitate the weekly sessions with the catechumens. I also coordinate the efforts of the team, and oversee the whole process. I have particular responsibility for developing materials for the catechumenal sessions and the scheduling of guest catechists. I also have the major responsibility for planning the liturgies in our parish, along with the celebrant and choir director.

3. *What is the most satisfying aspect of your ministry?*

It is hard for me to say what is most satisfying. I suppose it would be the aspect that I am continually challenged by the catechumens. I find myself more conscious of the life I am living. Like it or not, I become a model for the catechumens. I am called to do what I ask them to do.

Especially as we reflect together on the Scriptures, and their meaning in our lives, I have to constantly see my own life in the light of these words, and feel the call to constant conversion, and the challenge to be more Christ-like.

4. *What advice would you give for others who will become catechumenate directors?*

First of all, I would tell them to relax. The job can seem overwhelming, but the Spirit is at work, and we ought to trust the Spirit as we do what we can to facilitate conversion.

Secondly, I would remind them not to look so much to the structures we might design, but to really concentrate on what is happening with the catechumens.

Pastor
Father Thomas Caroluzza, Our Lady of Nazareth Parish
Roanoke, Virginia

1. *How is your parish organized for the RCIA?*

We have a parish team that includes a director for the catechumenate, a coordinator of sponsors, a coordinator of fellowship events, three spiritual directors, a secretary, a coordinator of catechists, a liturgy planner, and the pastor (or one of the parish priests). There are committees of the team that do some of the specific work, such as planning for the liturgical rites.

2. *Describe your responsibilities as pastor in the RCIA.*

Over the nine years that we have been doing the catechumenate, my role has been continually changing and developing. A major aspect has always been enabling others to minister in the catechumenate. As team membership shifts, some members need more help than others, and it is a major concern of mine that all have the support

they need to enable them to minister effectively in their roles.

Often, I am called on to pinch-hit for someone else, and in that capacity, I will serve as catechist occasionally, or fill in temporarily in some other capacity.

The on-going work of planning and evaluating is an important aspect of the team's work, and an important aspect of my role with them.

I also have special responsibility during the interviews, working on individual growth plans, and spiritual direction. I am not sure if this will be an enduring role or not, but it has been important up to this point. Of course, celebrating the rites is a major role, and that calls me to work closely with the liturgy planners.

3. *What is the most satisfying aspect of your ministry?*

The individual contact I can have with people is the single most satisfying thing. It is truly a privilege to be part of such an intense experience in people's lives, to watch them go through conversion, and see changes happening in them.

The liturgical rites are powerful experiences for me also, largely because of that deep relationship we have developed. One year, I decided not to be part of the catechumenate team, but simply to celebrate the rites, and it was horrible. The opportunity to really celebrate out of a relationship is so much better.

4. *What advice would you give for others who will be the pastor on the catechumenate team?*

I would advise them to be journeyers themselves. People don't need us to know everything, or to be everything for them. They need us to journey with them through this process.

Also, I advise them to jump right into the process, and not wait until all is perfectly planned; it will all come together, as long as we are open to growth and change.

Catechist
Sister Mary Ann Hartnett, St. Ambrose Parish
Baltimore, Maryland

1. *How is your parish organized for the RCIA?*

At our parish, when I began working as catechist, there was already an organized structure which I had to build on, and a planned catechesis that I was able to continue to use. We are working more on building our team now. At this point we have six people on our team—one of our priests is the director of the process, and I am the catechist; one other member does all the record keeping and paper work; another makes the phone calls and direct personal contacts; and two other members coordinate the sponsors.

2. *Describe your responsibilities as catechist.*

I am responsible for all the teaching; most of it I do myself, but I am also responsible to share it with other appropriate people. I develop the curriculum; make sure that I am well prepared, both professionally and spiritually. I take care of the schedule for the process in the parish, prepare materials needed, and have the handouts available. I also funnel all necessary information to the other team members.

3. *What is the most satisfying aspect of your ministry?*

My full time ministry at the parish is teaching children in the school. Other than that, I have to say that I find the RCIA is the most fulfilling experience that I have had. It is hard to explain, but as we begin with each new group, the feeling is not "Here we go again," but a real feeling of beginning a journey with the people. Each time, I can see the growth happening; I can watch the togetherness happen, and really see the grace of God at work.

The term faith community may be overused, but it really fits here. We always have such a varied group, but all of them, catechumens, sponsors, parishioners, all form into a real community around the Spirit of God. You can see that it must be God. As you hear people tell their story, you can hear the progress they are making. Each evening when I leave, I am so "up." I have such a good feeling. It is so true here that "By your students you are taught." I can just go on and on about how satisfying this ministry is, but what I say is really sincere.

4. *What advice would you give for others who will become catechists?*

First, I would say, don't be afraid, go ahead and be one. It is a very fulfilling experience. If you feel called, don't be afraid that you won't know how. Some nights, I have all my plans, I am all ready . . . then the Spirit really is the one who does the teaching. I wonder where it comes from. So don't be afraid, but do be open to the Spirit.

It's not a matter of "anything goes," of course. The catechist must be prepared, both academically and spiritually. The function of catechist is key to the work of the whole team.

5. *As catechist, would you say something about the concern for curriculum?*

Curriculum is very important. It just cannot be a matter of hit and miss. We have a well developed curriculum that includes the major elements of the faith, and we present the whole in view of conversion. It is not so tight that there is no deviation, but it is a definite curriculum. We know that we do not teach everything, but we have a real sense of where we are going. We always put Scripture at the beginning because conversion is to the Lord, and the stories of Scripture put that in perspective. I believe the catechist has a special responsibility to be aware of the curriculum, and to be constantly evaluating it.

Interview with a Sponsor
Denise McCord, Corpus Christi Parish
Baltimore, Maryland

1. *Describe your responsibilities as a sponsor.*

The main role was to be a support for the candidates. The sponsor was always there for them to answer questions, or direct them to others who could answer their questions. The idea was that they would really know someone in this parish. We would always be with them on Sunday, and at other parish functions.

Sponsors were invited to all the catechetical sessions, and we came to just about all of them. It helped us to get to know the person, and we usually had questions to ask about the topic, and much to learn along with the candidate.

We also were active in all the rites, and frequently were asked to speak on behalf of the candidates.

2. *How was the match made between sponsor and candidate?*

I really think it was the Holy Spirit!

The group met for three or four months over the summer before sponsors became part of the process. The leaders were getting to know the people, and finding out what they wanted, and the people were finding out what they could expect.

Then all the sponsors and candidates got together for a dinner, where we could meet one another; after that, the team made the matches. All of them turned out well. It just couldn't have worked out better. Most of the candidates didn't know anyone here before that, and now there is a real friendship between sponsor and candidate, and with the rest of the group as well.

3. Tell me about the person you sponsored.

She was a nurse, already baptized. Her family didn't understand her wanting to be Catholic, and they had some strong anti-Catholic feelings. She had a million questions, and some doubts, but she was just so determined to become a member. I admired her so much.

Now I always look for her at church on Sunday, and we talk outside of that as well. It happened that my mother died of cancer during the time I was involved in the RCIA, and Barbara's father had died with the same form of cancer. She was such a help and support to me. Perhaps it was a coincidence, but it seems to me that we were really chosen to be together. She is very special to me.

So is the rest of the group. Even my son (who is 5 years old) knows them, and feels close to them. It mirrors the feeling of what Corpus Christi really is, a place for all ages, a mixed group, a true welcoming place.

4. What advice would you give to someone who is asked to be a sponsor?

Definitely, do it! For me, being a sponsor was a true faith experience. It does require a real commitment—of time, but even more, a commitment of yourself to someone else. But you receive much more than you give. On Holy Saturday, after initiation, it was sheer joy to see them go down the aisle, sprinkling the rest of the congregation. I felt like a child at Christmas. All the Tuesday nights were worth it!

For me personally, I had always kind of envied the catechumens. Now I had the chance to be with them, traveling together on this faith journey. I didn't even think of saying no. It was a real time of growth in spirit, and a faith filled experience. I would definitely do it again!

5. What advice would you give for RCIA teams as they choose and train sponsors?

First, make sure you look for people who don't think they have all the answers.

Remember too that sponsors should be given a chance to have input in evaluating, and designing changes that should be made for future years. They can point out things that didn't go as well as they could.

Finally, be sure that you let people know what will really be expected of them. At our parish, we had a meeting for a large number of people, to acquaint them with the idea of sponsor, and what would be expected of them if they agreed to take on the role. Many of that group said no, but those who agreed to say yes were really prepared for what was ahead.

TEAM TASKS
1. Overall planning: program design and schedule
2. Budgeting
3. Evaluating
4. Developing and forming leadership

Team tasks:
1. Overall Planning—Program Design and Schedule

- What is the basic plan for the whole process?
- When will you schedule major liturgical rites?
- What minor rites should be scheduled, and when?
- What is your beginning date?
- When will participation be closed to new members?
- What options can you make available to participants?
- What parish events, or other church events, should be part of your schedule?
- With whom should you consult as you plan your schedule?
- How will this schedule become part of the parish calendar?
- How will you publicize it?
- How will you make your schedule flexible enough to serve the needs of individuals?

2. Budgeting

Items to consider
Salaries
Stipends for guest speakers
Rental or purchase of audio-visual materials
Books or periodicals for catechumens
Support materials for team and sponsors
Hospitality needs
Space
Transportation
Publicity
Liturgical needs
Library
Equipment
Gifts or awards

Questions

- Should you charge participants anything?
- Where does the RCIA fit in your parish budget?

3. Evaluating

Thoughts about evaluation

Evaluation can help both leaders and participants. It helps leaders as they plan for the future. Looking carefully at what has been done and how it worked should be a major part of future decisions. It helps participants look at their own experience and identify what is happening for them.

Some guidelines for evaluation
1. Evaluate only when necessary. Everything does not need to be evaluated.
2. The evaluation should be simple and easy to complete.
3. Don't ask unnecessary questions. Have a reason for what you do ask.
4. Make sure you use the evaluation responses.
5. Always have space for comments.
6. Both leaders and participants have valuable evaluative contributions to make.
7. Both objective and subjective language are useful. Rating scales are often helpful.

Sample Evaluation Form

Was today's program helpful in meeting your needs?

5   4   3   2   1

Very helpful . . . . Not helpful at all

What did you find most helpful?

What was least helpful for you?

---

4. Developing and Forming Leaders

Considerations about recruiting volunteers
1. Is a face-to-face conversation used for asking persons to serve in a volunteer ministry?
2. Are persons being asked to take on a job given a written description of what they are being asked to do?
3. Is everyone who is asked to participate in volunteer ministry given an accurate picture of how much time and effort it will take to carry it out?
4. Is everyone who is asked to participate in a volunteer ministry given information about what he or she needs to know in order to do the ministry well?
5. Have all parish members been given a choice in volunteer ministry positions?
6. Are persons told why they were chosen to be asked to undertake a particular volunteer ministry?

Considerations about training volunteers
1. Before people take on new positions do they participate in an orientation session?
2. Is there some way for persons who have completed a position to pass on helpful information to the persons who take over the positions?
3. Are learning opportunities provided members as they carry out volunteer ministry?
4. Does your parish sponsor retreats, Bible study or specific courses designed to help volunteers develop new skills and knowledge?
5. Does your parish pay for members to attend training sessions outside the Church?
6. Are all ministry positions currently filled by people adequately trained to do them?

Considerations about supporting volunteers
1. Do all volunteers receive orientation and training for their tasks so that they can go about them with confidence and work effectively?
2. Do all volunteers know there is someone available to assist and encourage them?
3. Generally, are parish members aware of persons doing volunteer ministry on their behalf in the community and beyond the local church?
4. Are volunteers recognized and thanked by the Church for their services?
5. Do volunteers have adequate resources to carry out their work?
6. Are records kept of the volunteer services of each member?

(Adapted from *The Ministry of Volunteers: A Guidebook for Churches,* Office for Church Life and Leadership of the United Church of Christ, Church Leadership Resources, P.O. Box 179, St. Louis, MO, 63166, 1979.)

Sample Program to Prepare Sponsors

Meeting #1
● Discuss past experience with being or having a sponsor or godparent.
● Present overview of the RCIA process and how it works in this particular parish.

- Point out the role of sponsor in this process. (A sponsor from past years may be the best person to explain this, and give personal witness.)
- Identify specific commitment asked of sponsors; ask each person to consider his/her ability to accept such a commitment at this time.

Meeting #2
Practice in faith sharing. (Reflect, then share significant faith experiences from the past, with one other person.)

Discuss:
> How does it feel to share deeply about faith?
> Do you remember what the other person said?
> How can you encourage another's sharing?

Are you ready to make the commitment to be a sponsor now?

Present the schedule for the coming year and discuss questions and possibilities.

On-going Support and Evaluation
Plan for regular individual informal contact with Sponsor Coordinator—"How are you doing?"

About one-third of the way through the process, meet for about one-half hour with catechumens and sponsors in separate groups, and ask for evaluation of the relationship, and suggestions for growth.

For a further resource on preparing sponsors, see:

Bacchi, Maureen, "The Ministry of the Spiritual Friend", *Chicago Catechumenate*, Vol. 6, No. 4.

PARISH WORKSHEET
1. What role will be played by your pastor?

2. Who will serve as catechumenate director?

3. Who will serve as primary catechist?

4. Who will coordinate the sponsors?

5. How will you attract inquirers?

6. What other roles do you need in your parish?
   Spiritual director? (Who will pay special attention to spiritual growth?)
   Liturgical planner? (Who will make plans and adaptions for your parish celebrations?)
   Hospitality? (Who will set up refreshments and be responsible for a friendly, welcoming spirit?)

7. How will the team relate to the Parish Council?

8. How will the team relate to other parish structures?

9. What kind of training will team members need? How will they get it?

10. What kind of on-going formation will team members need? How will they get it?

11. What resources do you need to work effectively? How will you get them?

12. How will you evaluate your work?

13. What will be your meeting schedule?

Chapter IV

The RCIA Experience: Precatechumenate

- Introducing the Period
- What the Document Says
- Meet the Inquirer
- Significant Issues in Precatechumenate
- Composite Model
- Other Models
- Parish Worksheet

INTRODUCING THE PERIOD:
EVANGELIZATION AND PRECATECHUMENATE

This period is called evangelization or precatechumenate. The two names refer to distinct yet related kinds of activities. Evangelization is the ministry of sharing the good news in such a way that attracts a person to respond with a desire to know more. Precatechumenate is the first ministering to those who respond.

Evangelization leads to:	Precatechumenate responds with:
"I want to find out more about the Lord."	"Come and see how we respond to the Lord in our community."
"I do believe in Jesus!"	"Our community can help you know Jesus better."
"I want some of what you have"	"Come let us grow in faith together
All people need evangelization, from active Catholics to the truly unchurched.	Precatechumenate activities focus on the needs of those who are unchurched, considering membership in the Catholic Church.

Evangelization and RCIA should be seen as partners in a parish. They are inter-dependent, and each ministry needs the other. Evangelizers and initiators should coordinate their efforts as well as understand and support one another's work.

About Evangelization

Evangelization: "Bringing the good news into all the strata of humanity, and, through its influence, transforming humanity from within, and making it new" ("On Evangelization in the Modern World", #18).

1. Evangelization ought to be seen as an essential part of every parish's life. It should be the natural impulse of every believer, and the sign of vitality of a parish family. It would be impossible to implement RCIA well in a parish that was not evangelizing.

2. Pope Paul VI, in his exhortation, "On Evangelization in the Modern World," says: "Evangelizing is in fact the grace and vocation proper to the church, her deepest identity. She exists in order to evangelize . . ." (#14); and "It is unthinkable that a person should accept the Word and give himself to the kingdom without becoming a person who bears witness to it and proclaims it in his turn" (#24).

3. Experience shows that parishes with evangelization committees are in a better position to effectively evangelize; usually, a representative of this committee will be a member of the parish RCIA team.

4. Evangelization efforts are both formal and informal, person to person and community based, planned and spontaneous. All people need to be evangelized, to be challenged to a deeper commitment. For active Cath-

olics, this is in the form of renewal, or spiritual re-awakening. For inactive Catholics, it is the call to reconsider membership in the Church. For those in other Christian churches, it is in the form of ecumenical dialogue. For those who believe in God but not in Jesus, it is inter-religious dialogue. And for those who are truly unchurched, it is the invitation to come to know Jesus, and to join a believing community.

For further reading, see:

Hoge, *Converts, Drop-outs, and Returnees*.

Pope Paul VI, "On Evangelization in the Modern World".

About Precatechumenate

Precatechumenate: The first taste of what the Catholic community has to offer; gives a sense of what it would be like to be a part of the Catholic faith tradition.

1. All of the precatechumenate should be characterized by a spirit of welcome, openness, and freedom. Getting to know and appreciate each person's story is essential both for the individual inquirer and for the group.

2. The period should include a clear and honest initial experience of the Catholic way of life.

3. The experiences in this period are basic in nature, and will all be developed in more depth in later periods. People have not yet made a commitment, and so participation is more fluid than in other periods.

4. The precatechumenate period prepares for the celebration of the rite of acceptance into the order of catechumens. The ministers, the sessions, the interviews and the other activities should enable persons to make the decision to become or not become a catechumen.

5. During this period, parish leaders should become aware of any potential problems such as invalid marriages or family opposition. They must recognize religious background, and discern what further formation for full membership is indicated.

6. A parish sponsor should be assigned to be a partner for the journey of conversion as soon as possible.

7. The basic catechetical method is storytelling—the story of each individual, the story of the helping ministers, and the story of Jesus and the Church.

8. At least one personal interview should take place near the end of the period to evaluate readiness to move to the catechumenate. An earlier interview is also helpful.

Time Frame: Not specified

Liturgical Celebrations: (all are optional in this period)
In formal rite of welcoming the inquirer (RCIA, #39)
Appropriate prayers (RCIA, #40)
Exorcisms or blessings (may be anticipated from the catechumenate period, RCIA, #40)

For further reading on the precatechumenate, see:

Boyack, *A Parish Guide to Adult Initiation*, Chap. 2.

Dunning, *New Wine, New Wineskins*, Chap. 3.

Kemp, *A Journey In Faith*, Chap. 2.

RCIA, #9–13.

WHAT THE DOCUMENT SAYS ABOUT PRECATECHUMENATE
(Numbers refer to the Introduction in the RCIA)

#1 The RCIA (and precatechumenate) assumes that participants are adults who have been evangelized. They are beginning on a path of conversion.

#4 The whole community is involved in and benefits from the RCIA (and precatechumenate).

#5 The RCIA responds to individual spiritual journeys and is flexible enough to meet individual needs.

#7.1 The first period involves evangelization and precatechumenate. It prepares for the celebration of the rite of becoming a catechumen.

#36 Evangelization is proclaiming Jesus, and calling for a response to Jesus.

#37 Initial conversion as understood in this period is twofold: it is turning *away* from sin, and turning *toward* God.

#38 (and #9.1) Many ministers are needed in this period, including families and groups from the parish.

#42 During this period, the Church is to introduce the basic fundamentals of Christian life. On the part of the inquirer, it is time for conceiving first faith, initial conversion, first repentance and first experiences of Christian community.

#43 (and #45) Sponsors are needed as soon as possible.

#47 The precatechumenate ends with the rite of acceptance into the order of catechumens. At that point, the inquirer becomes a catechumen and is joined to the Church, "a part of the household of Christ".

#18 The rite of acceptance should be celebrated after a sufficient time for precatechumenate. It may be celebrated two or three times a year if necessary.

#43 Interviews are needed during precatechumenate.

#67 After the rite of acceptance, those preparing for membership should be dismissed after the Liturgy of the Word.

MEET THE INQUIRER

Below are listed some of the kinds of statements ministers hear in precatechumenate sessions. They indicate the great variety of people who respond to the invitation to learn more about the Catholic Church, or to talk about Jesus in their life. Whatever ways the parish uses to advertise for precatechumenate, people will come from very different backgrounds, and for very different reasons. The parish must be ready to begin anew with all new persons, listen respectfully to their story, and then begin the journey that helps them respond to Jesus's call for them.

"I know Jesus and want to come to know him better. Can you help me?"

"My family is Catholic. I want us to go to church together."

"I like your church. I think I want to join."

"I went to a novena." "I want to learn to say the rosary." "I pray to St. Jude." "I want holy water."

"I don't know why I am here, but I felt I should come and see what you have to offer."

"I feel lost and alone. My friend said maybe you could help me."

"I am new in the neighborhood, and this is the closest church."

"I just got divorced, and I want to start a new life."

SIGNIFICANT ISSUES IN EVANGELIZATION/ PRECATECHUMENATE

Flexibility

The flexibility that must characterize all RCIA ministry is first experienced and most challenging to accomplish in the precatechumenate period. The most obvious flexibility has to do with time. The team must be able to welcome and accept people whenever they come. No one should be asked to wait. No one should be forced to hurry up.

This issue is at the heart of the difference between viewing RCIA as a program and seeing it as a process guided by the conversion experience in individual lives. If it is a program, there is a beginning date, and those who come early do indeed need to wait; and there is an ending date, and those who come too late need to hurry up. Even our efforts to "make up classes" can really be an expression of a program mentality.

If, on the other hand, the RCIA is a process, then whenever a person experiences conversion graces, we can say, "Thank you, God, and welcome, Friend", and really mean it.

Experience makes it clear that a significant key to having a truly flexible RCIA is a truly flexible precatechumenate. Practically, this means that precatechumenate activity needs to be on-going throughout the year, so that whenever a person is ready to begin, the parish ministry is ready for him or her.

A parish can expect that most inquirers will come when you invite them to come—that is, in response to your major evangelization outreaches during the year. Precatechumenate activities should certainly be in high gear at those times. But some real and purposeful response must be available both for those who come at other times, and for those who would benefit from staying in precatechumenate for a longer period.

As a parish begins to implement RCIA, precatechumenate may be the most difficult period to get a handle on for the first year or so. Remember, it need not be perfect to be good; a parish should expect to learn by doing; and it is better to get started with something than to spend too long planning with nothing. The important thing is that a parish not be satisfied with its precatechumenate experience until it is really individualized and flexible.

Some ideas that may help to achieve flexibility in a precatechumenate are:

- Have sponsors and spiritual directors available for new inquirers throughout the year.
- Identify a precatechumenate coordinator who is able to concentrate on precatechumenate issues throughout the year.

- Be open to celebrate the rite of becoming a catechumen more than once a year.
- Clearly understand how to separate precatechumenate activities from catechumenate activities. In some cases, a person can do some precatechumenate sharing and decision making while sharing some other things with catechumens.

Openness to All

Evangelization and precatechumenate must be open to all people. Some people will come who perhaps do not belong in the RCIA; some who are apparently not called to membership in the Catholic Church; or some who are living a lifestyle that appears to be in opposition to the teaching of Jesus. All are to be welcome in the precatechumenate period. The only criterion at this point is a desire to come.

It is during the precatechumenate period that decisions are made. It is appropriate that there are some people who do not move into catechumenate; some who do not move into the enlightenment period. But it is not appropriate that anyone who wants to be included would be kept out of precatechumenate.

For some people, the decision may be to remain at the level of precatechumenate commitment for a long period of time, while moral questions or problems of faith are dealt with. Others may have specific difficulties that would call for some other form of ministry in addition to or in place of precatechumenate ministry (such as annulment proceedings or formal counseling). For some people who are already Catholic, alternate journeys (such as personal renewal programs or adult formation programs or retreats) might be indicated.

The precatechumenate will always be a messy period. People will be coming in and out; participants will be at different levels of faith and experience; deep questions of meaning will be discussed at the same time as peripheral issues of religious practices. Precatechumenate is where the welcome to all is lived out; where community is formed in the face of great diversity; where individual inquirers are met, understood, and accepted. Some ideas to help assure openness to all during this period are:

- Assign greeters for new people, who begin the process of integration and storytelling as each new person arrives.
- Schedule a formal interview with each person so that problems can be identified and procedures begun to deal with problems early on.
- Be serious about doing good publicity. Circulate invitations widely for activities during precatechumenate time. Make it clear that people are really welcome.

Models for Precatechumenate

Each of the models that follow describes how precatechumenate happened in a particular parish. Putting experience into words is always limited. Much of the personal contact, individual attention and hospitality touches do not come through in a written description. Remember that the purpose of including these models is to give a clearer picture of how the work of RCIA does happen in parishes, and how it reflects the gifts and needs of the individual community.

Composite Model

The Composite Model shows a beginning precatechumenate. Its best aspects are the activities surrounding the more formal sessions that take place. Note especially the liturgical celebrations and attention to spiritual life that happen during the process. The sessions highlight significant aspects of what it means to be Catholic, and have the benefit of building the beginning community that will be essential during the RCIA process. A primary problem is that it does have specific scheduled meetings which can take on the feeling of a class rather than the storytelling experience they should be. An especially sensitive group leader or facilitator is needed.

St. Augustine Parish Model

St. Augustine's model is on a second level of RCIA development. Though it still centers on group sessions, there is much more sensitivity to opening the process at any time. Parish involvement is high, and individual needs are directly addressed. The excellent Scripture foundation becomes a good basis for the rest of the process as well.

Household Model

This model shows a highly developed precatechumenate. Leadership for it comes naturally from among persons who have been sponsors in the past, and it may well be the precatechumenate of a parish's second or third year rather than the first.

Its best aspects are its flexibility and its ownership by the parish. People are really welcome whenever they arrive. It is very possible for someone to be finished with precatechumenate in less than two months, or to be in it in a productive way for over a year. Inquirers who go through this process have not only experienced storytelling, parish leadership and some catechesis, but in a very real sense have experienced several families in the parish, and know the community in a much better way than most other models can provide.

The model needs considerable planning so that people are not lost in the process, and that they are called to become a catechumen when they are ready. The roles of sponsor (even if it is a temporary sponsor) and the precatechumenate coordinator are key in this model.

COMPOSITE MODEL: PRECATECHUMENATE

Liturgical Celebrations
- Altar calls, "Opening the doors of the Church" (These terms are common among many Christian communities. They refer to a specific invitation to respond to Jesus in some way. The priest or other minister calls interested persons to come forward and prayers are offered for them, often while a hymn is being sung. This can be done appropriately after the homily or at the end of Mass. In this model, it was done on two separate Sundays, in late May and in August.)
- Formal blessing, and beginning of weekly dismissal third week of September. (Note that this model begins dismissal a few weeks before the rite of acceptance into the order of catechumens.)

Parish Life
- Personal invitation to special parish events—Homecoming Sunday, Fellowship Sunday, Healing Service, Bus Trips.
- Sponsors participating in sessions, with a view to assigning an appropriate match by the middle of August. Phone calls and informal visits by sponsors during this time.

Broader Church Awareness
- Discussion of major news events involving the Church in some way during the sessions.

Attention to Spiritual Life
- Focus in meetings on understanding personal story; recognizing and legitimizing personal spiritual experiences.
- Sponsors pay special attention to helping individuals recognize growth and facilitating personal storytelling.
- Talking about different types of prayer; specific prayer time in each session, with time for shared prayer.
- Interview before becoming a catechumen with the catechumenate director.

Social Ministry
- None at this point.

Meetings
- Scheduled monthly from May through September
- See following sheets for overview of sessions.

Composite Model: Precatechumenate Sessions

Session #1 (usually scheduled in May): **We Need One Another**

Purpose
To highlight the need for community in faith.

Major Points
- By nature, we need one another; we cannot survive alone.
- Experiences of community and aloneness usually are the experiences that call us to growth.
- God deals with us as individuals and calls us to community.
- The community challenges us, teaches us, enables us to share, gives us deeper experiences of God.
- Each of us should feel a call to some kind of community.
- Knowledge of the Trinity tells us that God is community.

What is Your Story?
- Discuss experiences of community.
  1. To what communities do you belong?
  2. Are they real communities?
  3. How do they affect us?

The Story of Jesus and the Church
- Presentation on community
  1. What we mean by community
  2. Human need for community
  3. Power of community (peer groups, civil rights movement)
  4. Americans and community; the danger of individualism
- God and community
  1. God formed a people for himself.
  2. He dealt with a whole family.
  3. Jesus called people to follow him, asked for individual commitment; then, he asked them to walk with him in community.
  4. There is no such thing as a Christian rugged individualist.
- Religions are the communities we join, as we feel led by God. We bond ourselves together, with Jesus. God always calls us to community. We need to discover the one to which God calls us.

How Does This Affect Your Story?
Are you feeling drawn to the Catholic community? Why?

Prayer

God is community. The Trinity is a mystery of our faith, which gives a hint to the importance of community for God. Our prayer is enhanced as we address God as Father, Son, Spirit.

Handout: *Invitation,* Chap. 3, McBride

Session #2 (usually scheduled in June): **Prayer**

Purpose

To help each person look at his/her prayer life, appreciate its value, and find directions for growth.

Major Points
- Prayer is the communication between God and you.
- Prayer is essential if we are to grow in faith.
- Each person's prayer is good where it is; each person's prayer needs to grow and expand.

What is Your Story?
- Share personal prayer life, using these reflection questions:
  1. Where do you feel you pray best?
  2. What time of day do you feel you pray best?
  3. Do you prefer to pray alone or with others?
  4. The one person who has had the greatest influence in my prayer life is. . . .
  5. The one thing my prayer life needs more of is. . . .

The Story of Jesus and the Church

What is prayer?

Prayer is our communication with God; *prayers* are those words we say to help us achieve it; the *pray-er* is the individual, the one who prays, and ultimately offers himself/herself to God. Point out personal nature of prayer and challenge of prayer.

How Does This Affect Your Story?
- Discuss the variety of ways we will be praying during the catechumenate process; welcome the challenge to test out some new forms of prayer (shared prayer, spontaneous prayer, formal prayer, meditative prayer, liturgical prayer).

Prayer
- Give out copies of Catholic Prayers for Everyday, and use some of those prayers together.

Handout: "Catholic Prayers for Everyday", Paulist Catholic Evangelization Association; *Invitation,* Chap. 26 (McBride)

Session #3 (usually scheduled in July): **The Bible in the Catholic Church**

Purpose

To present the importance of Scripture in the Catholic community; to encourage regular reading of Scripture.

Major Points
- Scripture is both a gift to and a product of the community.
- Interpretation of Scripture should be based on the whole experience of God and how God acts with people.
- Personal knowledge and use of Scripture is a responsibility for every Christian.

What is Your Story?
- Discuss: What are your feelings about Scripture?
  1. What are your main questions about Scripture?
  2. Do you have a favorite story, or quote, or character in Scripture?

The Story of Jesus and the Church
- Look at the book itself, and point out what it is: Old and New Testaments, variety of books and styles of writing; discuss translations; explain "Catholic Bible" and "Protestant Bible".
- It is really a book of faith, the inspired Word of God. Writers, copiers, translators, readers—all were, and must be, people of faith to understand it. Prayer should always be part of our approach to Scripture.

How Does This Affect Your Story?
- Give out copies of the Bible for personal use (preferably the New American Bible, because it is the translation used in most official Catholic liturgies and publications).
- Point out the gospels, and highlight their importance in the whole book. Give some indication of how they differ and how they are alike.
- Assist each inquirer in choosing one gospel to read as a whole over the next several weeks. Encourage a regular reading pattern, real study, and openness to hear the message.
  1. What does it say?
  2. How does it fit into the story?
  3. What does it mean for me now?

Prayer
- Point out use of Scripture at Mass, and show how to find readings that will be used the coming Sunday. Use those readings as a basis for shared prayer to close the session.

Handout: New American Bible
            The Bible and You, Scriptographics
            pamphlet.
            Current issue of Share the Word

Session #4 (usually scheduled in August): **The Church is Catholic**

Purpose

To respond to questions about Catholic practices; to give an appreciation of the pluralism in the Church.

Major Points

- An opportunity to address issues raised around traditionally Catholic things such as the Pope, priestly celibacy, statues, devotions to Mary.
- Tradition of pluralism in our history—variety in styles of worship, inclusion of all kinds of people, experiences of diversity.
- Emphasize our overall unity in Eucharist.

What is Your Story?

- Discuss: What do you think of when you hear the word "Catholic"?
  1. What things do you think of as specifically Catholic?
  2. What questions do you have about Catholic things? (Try to get questions raised first, then begin answering. Some questions, however, need quick, definitive answers—"Why do Catholics worship Mary?"—"We don't. We honor her because of her special role, but we worship only God.")

The Story of Jesus and the Church

- Answer main areas of questions in an in-depth way. For instance, area of Mary and the saints: use examples, and give underlying reasons for use of saints as models; present some of the familiar prayers of saints, and intercessory prayer to saints.
  For instance, area of authority: give need for authority in preserving the message of Jesus, biblical examples of the apostles' role; and modern statements of infallibility; include individual conscience responsibility, and the role and existence of dissent.
- Be sure to really answer each question—many times, a specific yes or no is needed before going into more explanation. Don't spend too much time on any one question; there should be many.
- If there is time, or if the participants aren't raising many questions, raise some you want to talk about:
  1. Do you know who our bishop is, and what he does?
  2. Do you know why Catholics are supposed to go to Mass every Sunday?
  3. Do you know what is special about our parish?

How Will This Affect Your Story?

- Close with a discussion of the word "catholic", and its origin for the Church. What will it mean to be part of a *catholic* Church? How will we accept "catholicity" and diversity, and still be united in faith? (Close with prayer)

Handout: *About Being Catholic*,
            Scriptographics

Session #5 (usually scheduled in September): **The Journey**

Purpose

To look at the reality of conversion, and see how it is really an on-going journey; to help inquirers in their decision about becoming a catechumen; explain dismissal.

Major Points

- The difference conversion makes; what it means to change.
- Ability to get in touch with our own conversion.
- Description of the RCIA, and what is possible at this point for them.

What is Your Story?

- Describe what is happening in your life. What makes you come to these meetings? What do you expect?

The Story of Jesus and the Church

- Use this input to talk about conversion. God initiates it; it means change; it is the same for all of us and it is different for all of us. Conversion happens on many levels. We change intellectually, emotionally, physically, in groups, in actions; religious conversion is a radical transformation of how we view ourselves, our world, our lives, because of God.
  We do not control conversion, we accept it, we live it, we treasure it, we enjoy it. We do it as "we"—together.
- The RCIA is the Catholic Church experiencing conversion with its new members.
- Describe the process, particularly dismissal and the rite of acceptance into the order of catechumens.

What effect does this have on your story?

- Discuss what it would mean to decide to become a catechumen at this time, and what options are available for people.

Prayer

   Handout: *Invitation*, Chap. 1 (McBride)

OTHER MODELS
The Evangelization/Precatechumenate Period
at Saint Augustine Parish, Washington D.C. (1982)
Catechumenate Director: John Butler

Our evangelization efforts come primarily from the whole parish. Our gospel choir attracts new people almost every Sunday. People who make appointments with parish priests, for various reasons, are often steered into the catechumenate, if it is appropriate. Those people are invited into the RCIA process throughout the year. We never ask anyone to wait.

Usually around March, when we are ready to begin the formal precatechumenate, we begin advertising in the bulletin and from the pulpit. The community is encouraged to invite friends and relatives to the process.

Where possible, we have an initial interview with each precatechumen before the process begins. This interview may be held with the priest who will be involved that year or the catechumenate director.

In March, all of the inquirers come together, both those who have been attending the catechumenate sessions, and those who are new. At the first meeting, we spend most of the time getting to know one another and filling out forms. Our particular interest at this point is to gather information regarding the previous church affiliation and marriage situations, so we might be alerted to potential problems.

Through the rest of the time of the precatechumenate, we focus on three dynamics:

1. Interacting with the parish;

2. Raising and answering questions about the community and the Church; and

3. Involving the participants in an initial look at Scripture, the Old Testament in particular.

We offer a basic introduction to Scripture, and literary form criticism early in the process so that our use of the Scripture is guided. We use the New American Bible and focus on its introduction, footnotes, and cross references, in teaching how to use the Bible.

One dynamic we use frequently during the process is called "the hot seat." It involves parishioners, usually leaders or heads of parish organizations, who are invited to attend a session, and share their faith journey with the inquirers. This introduces the model of storytelling, as well as introducing the inquirer to what is going on in the parish, and some of the people in the parish.

We also have small groups of three to five people sharing with one another. To encourage as much trust and participation as possible, the subject matter is non-threatening.

Any given session may involve all three dynamics, or one may take the whole time that week. We always start each session by addressing questions from the inquirers. Any material to be covered is second to their request.

In addition to the New American Bible, we give copies of Kohmescher's *Catholicism Today*, and assign readings in it during the precatechumenate. This usually forms the basis of the questions that will be raised about the Church.

Sessions are scheduled on Wednesday evenings from March through July. August is the time for vacations, and participants are encouraged to attend other parishes during that time, either in the city, or wherever they might be. In September, our first order of discussion is what they experienced in these visits.

By this time, sponsors have been prepared to assume their role. We have four sessions for them. They focus on their own spiritual journeys, their ability to relate with others, their ministry in the parish, their personal strengths and their gifts. The team discusses appropriate matches for the sponsors, and by the end of September, they are assigned to their catechumens. In the future, our intention is to do this earlier, and have the sponsors in place before the August break.

A second interview, or discernment period, is held at the end of this pre-catechumenate period. We attempt to discern real motivations, to identify what initially brought them to the process, and what they are seeking now.

The rite of acceptance into the order of catechumens is held in middle or late October, and dismissal begins at that point, and continues throughout the catechumenate.

Evangelization/Precatechumenate Model
Based on Catechumenal Households
Five catechumenal households are needed in this plan:

1. An introductory household (usually the home of the coordinator of the period)

2. Scripture household

3. Prayer household

4. Catholic practice household

5. Parish contact household

Larger parishes may need more households. For instance there may be three or four prayer households, with referrals made on the basis of neighborhood.

Introductory Household

- First meeting: sharing personal faith stories; getting to know the individual inquirer, so that a sponsor can be temporarily assigned, and a plan of growth designed.
- Second meeting: with possible sponsor, assessing needs, and discussing probable growth plan. This will usually include some planned contact with each of the five other households. It may also include checking back for evaluation and more direction if desired.

Scripture Household

- Basic experience: showing how to use Scripture; explaining the plan of Sunday readings, and the lectionary; encouraging inquirers to begin reading the Bible regularly; dealing with principles of interpretation in a general way.
- Additional sessions may be scheduled to increase facility with using Scripture, or to study some sections together in more depth.

Prayer Household

- Basic experience: sharing about personal prayer lives; spending time in prayer together; offering an invitation to call at other times for prayer, or to come again for a visit and prayer.
- Additional meetings could be scheduled with other households involved in other prayer styles, so that formal prayer, charismatic prayer, and shut-ins with a spirit of prayer are also experienced.
- Many inquirers begin to visit on a regular basis for prayer, and begin to meet other inquirers who are doing the same thing.

Catholic Practice Household

- Basic experience: sharing a few of the specifically "Catholic" practices that have been helpful for this family; inviting the specific questions the inquirer has, and giving appropriate answers.
- Additional meetings may be scheduled if an inquirer has difficulties with something Catholic. This household might also arrange visits to other parish churches, or Catholic institutions in the area. Visits should usually be made with a sponsor, or some responsible guide or interpreter.

Parish Contact Household

- Basic experience: to explain the offerings of the parish; to arrange meetings and activities with others in the parish; to invite inquirers to specific events of interest in the parish.

In addition to these meetings, the sponsor and/or a catechumenal household arranges an interview with the priest or catechumenate director when the person seems ready to become a catechumen.

These activities may or may not be supplemented with group sessions on the same topics, with a catechist and facilitator as leader. People who have been to the households are usually quite ready to share, and now have deeper experiences and questions that have become part of their story.

This model can meet individual needs from one extreme to the other. For instance, for already baptized and catechized persons, part of the decision process in the first two meetings may lead to being received into the Church without a specific catechumenate process.

For some other people, several months may be needed in this period; they may move on to begin catechumenate meeting along with others, but need the personal attention of this kind of activity for a longer period. They may become catechumens in December, or just before Lent, and then go on to become elect.

PARISH WORKSHEET

1. How will you design your precatechumenate period?

2. Who is being attracted by your parish evangelization efforts? What are their religious needs?

3. What topics will you address in the precatechumenate period to meet these needs?

4. How many sessions will you need to accomplish this?

5. When will you schedule them?

6. Who will be the ministers from your community for this period?

7. Who will lead the meetings?

8. Who will recruit participants?

9. Who will do the interviews for the inquirer?

10. What options will you make available for those who choose to wait to become a catechumen? How will you respond to those who come early or late?

Chapter V

The RCIA Experience: Catechumenate

■ Introducing the Period
■ What the Document Says
■ Meet the Catechumen
■ Significant Issues in Catechumenate
■ Composite Model
■ Other Models
■ Parish Worksheet

INTRODUCING THE PERIOD: CATECHUMENATE

Catechumenate: A well-rounded experience of what it means to be Catholic, including an understanding of our faith, and an adult experience of it.

1. The experience of the period focuses on the Word of God proclaimed in the worshiping community, and then shared among catechumens after dismissal.

2. The catechesis is to follow the guidelines in the National Catechetical Directory, and should include aspects of all catechesis: message, community, service, worship.

3. The learning experiences should be guided by principles of adult learning.

4. Liturgical rites should be celebrated to encourage the catechumens along the journey.

5. Signs of parish membership are important during this period. Catechumens should be on the parish mailing list, receive the diocesan newspaper, begin membership in committees and other parish groups and have offertory envelopes.

6. The nature of the catechumenate flows from the rite of becoming a catechumen, and leads to the rite of election. Catechumens are now joined to the Church.

However, they retain freedom throughout the period to leave, or to extend the time they spend in the catechumenate. By becoming a catechumen a person does assume a commitment to the whole of the catechumenate process. He or she is expected to experience the period in its entirety in order to make an informed decision regarding the celebration of the rite of election.

7. In addition to the on-going responsibilities of sponsors and other ministers of initiation, the roles of catechist and spiritual director(s) take on special significance. The catechist regularly reviews the curriculum so that the message of our faith is presented in an adequate manner; and the spiritual director assures individual attention to the action of God within each catechumen and candidate.

8. At least one personal interview should occur towards the end of this period. It is to be a significant time for discernment, when the readiness of each catechumen for the rite of election must be evaluated. When problems are evident, they should be discussed early in the catechumenate, while there is adequate time for working them out.

Time Frame: Not specified; must be long enough to give an adequate experience of what it means to be Catholic.

Liturgical Celebrations:
Rite of acceptance into the order of catechumens

(RCIA #48–74)
Dismissal (RCIA #67)
Celebrations of the Word of God (RCIA #81–89)
Blessings (RCIA #95–97)
Exorcisms (RCIA # 90–94)

To learn more about this period, see:

RCIA, Introduction #41, 42, 47, 75–80.

Boyack, *A Parish Guide*, Chap. 3.

Dunning, *New Wine, New Wineskins*, Chap. 4.

Kemp, *Journey in Faith*, Chap. 3.

WHAT THE DOCUMENT SAYS ABOUT CATECHUMENATE

#4 and #5 (Applicable in each period of the RCIA) The whole community is involved in and benefits from the RCIA. The RCIA responds to individual spiritual journeys and is flexible enough to meet individual needs.

#7.2 The catechumenate begins with the rite of becoming a catechumen, and ends with the rite of election. It may last for several years. It is the time for complete catechesis.

#75.1 The catechumenate is to include the *message:* a suitable knowledge of dogma and precepts.

#75.2 The catechumenate is to include the experience and witness of the Christian *community:* it is a time of transition, and change should be evident.

#75.3 The catechumenate is to include liturgical rites, celebrations of the Word, and other opportunities for prayer and *worship.* Ordinarily dismissal should be a regular part of formation.

#75.4 The catechumenate is to include apostolic work with the community, experiencing from the beginning that Church membership involves *service.*

#76 The length of the catechumenate depends on a variety of circumstances, including those of the catechumens and the local church, and on the grace of God. It cannot be predetermined.

#76 The catechumenate continues until the catechumens are sufficiently mature. It is the time for experiencing the whole of the Christian life.

#78 The whole of Catholic teaching is to be included, and apostolic action is to be fostered.

#81 Instructions should follow the liturgical year. (Indicates using the lectionary to guide the catechumenate.)

#90 The exorcisms are to teach catechumens that the struggle against evil is part of the spiritual life.

#95 The blessings are signs of the love of God and the care of the Church to encourage catechumens along their spiritual journey.

#122 There must be an opportunity for discernment towards the end of the period to determine readiness to celebrate the rite of election.

MEET THE CATECHUMEN

Below are listed some of the kinds of statements ministers hear during the catechumenate. It is a time for listening for the signs of conversion that should become evident during this period. Catechumens cannot always identify what is happening to them, but something should be happening. Recognizing those changes, and God's part in them, is an important part of helping the catechumen during this time.

"At work, I keep struggling to deal with some really difficult people. I feel like Moses, and I wonder why God is making Pharaoh so obstinate."

"I don't go to dances as much as I used to. I used to get in trouble when I did, and now I just decide to do other things with my time."

"My family tells me that I have changed. I don't get so upset the way I used to. Instead, I just pray a little, trust in Jesus, and do what I have to do."

"I am starting to feel a little better about myself. I never thought I had anything to offer. Since I've been coming here, though, I see that I have been able to help some other people, and I see that there are others who feel the same way I do about things."

"Sometimes, God just seems to be too good to be true. Is it really possible?"

SIGNIFICANT ISSUES IN CATECHUMENATE

Catechesis

Catechumenate, catechism, catechist, catechesis, all have the same root word, the Greek "katekeo" which reflects a sounding, a personal communication. It describes the action of sharing the faith we have received from others. It is an appropriate word for the action of the catechumenate—passing on faith, which others have passed on to us.

The word has often been misunderstood to mean only teaching information. Recent Church documents have gone to great lengths to broaden the meaning of the term from that limited view. "To Teach As Jesus Did" described three necessary aspects for catechesis: message, community, and service. The National Catechetical Directory, *Sharing the Light of Faith*, expands that to include a fourth aspect of catechesis, worship. (Paragraphs #39, 215, 218, 227)

These documents, along with the experience of Church tradition, and even the witness of common sense, tell us that simply teaching content is not adequately passing on faith. The RCIA reminds us of the same thing in different words. We cannot share the Christian life without sharing experiences of community, service and worship. Neither can we adequately share the Christian life without the message.

Much discussion centers on the issue of content in the RCIA. While there is a variety of opinions on how the content of the faith should be communicated, all agree that it is an essential part of the catechumenate. Certainly we need to include content in the RCIA; but certainly it is not everything.

The catechesis in the RCIA, as all catechesis, must follow the guidelines set by the National Catechetical Directory. It must include message, community, service, and worship, or it is not good catechesis. This is true not only for adults in the catechumenate, but for every person growing in faith, from a young child to an adult.

Some ideas that may help to achieve full catechesis in the catechumenate are:

- Call catechumens to experience a variety of opportunities for personal service during the catechumenate. Appropriate activities would be projects like preparing and delivering Christmas baskets, or other projects for the poor; cleaning house or minor home repairs for elderly or infirm neighbors; visiting the sick or prisons; tutoring children; attending community improvement meetings, writing letters to members of congress or state legislators.

- Instill and build real community among catechumens. Make sure they know one another's names and care about one another. Design sessions so that discussion is not between teacher and learner, but usually among learners with a facilitator drawing out, pointing direction, and identifying significant insights.

- Schedule social events, and encourage friendly relationships beyond planned activities. Coffee breaks and hospitality times are essential parts of catechumenate sessions.

- Treat the period of sharing after dismissal as a holy time. It continues the worship experience of the Liturgy of the Word, and it should feel like a privileged time.

Curriculum

The document directs that the team have a curriculum for the catechumenate period. It speaks of a plan of instruction, the period of study. Designing an appropriate curriculum is key in developing a good catechumenate.

The difficulty is that getting a curriculum for the catechumenate is not the same process as getting a curriculum for a specific grade level or sacrament preparation program. This curriculum must include all the essential elements of our faith; it must respond to needs, interests, and gifts of individual participants; and its goal is the faith response of the whole person, rather than providing specific information.

The RCIA team, specifically the primary catechist, must be sure that catechumens have the opportunity to hear all the essential elements of our faith. They do not have to learn everything we teach. They do not have to remember everything they learn. What is significant is their experience of conversion, not their knowledge. But RCIA leaders have to do their part in presenting the faith in the best way possible.

Here are two suggestions about how to develop a curriculum for your parish:

(1) Involve the catechetical leadership of the parish in a process that leads to development of a curriculum that is unique to the parish. The goal is to make the curriculum a real statement of the faith of the whole Church, as well as the faith of this parish. The plan described here would require a one day or an extended morning workshop with the key people in the parish. This should include at least the RCIA team, CCD teachers and education committees; it would be well to include many others—music ministers, liturgy committee members, Parish Council, staff people, etc.

Step #1 Introduction to the day, including a presentation on the meaning of catechesis as sharing faith, and our need to be able to verbalize faith.

Step #2 Ask each person to reflect individually on what is at the heart of the Catholic faith for him or her. Individually, list those things that must be included if you are to share what it means to be Catholic. (Allow about 20 minutes for such personal reflection.)

Step #3 Have participants share these thoughts in small groups of four or five people. Each is to share his or her list; then begin the process of organizing the elements into groups. These more organized lists are then to be written on newsprint, ready to be presented to the total group. This should take about 45 minutes.

Step #4 As the groups make their presentation to one another, two things happen: First, there is some level of surprise that the lists are so much alike (of course, they should be; we do share the same faith); second, groups are surprised at what they forgot, and others remembered. (We need one another to be Church fully.)

Step #5 The next task is to bring together the separate lists, combine and rearrange the elements so that there is a fairly complete statement of our faith, organized in a reasonable manner. This step takes about 45 minutes.

Step #6 As a closing activity, the group should focus on deciding what is most important, and what is of secondary importance. Of all the pieces, one or two elements should stand out as having unique significance. These are the truly unifying aspects of our faith that deserve a clearly primary position in all our teaching.

The final work is done by just a few people (probably the primary catechist for the RCIA and the DRE for the parish). They must evaluate the outline, to see that it is an adequate one. It should be measured first against chapter five of the National Catechetical Directory, entitled, "Essential Teachings of the Catholic Faith", to assure that all of the essential elements are included. Then, it should be measured against at least two good adult catechisms or learning guides, to see if there are other aspects that should be included that are not.

These people next take this raw material, and fill out the curriculum design for the catechumenate. It has been organized in a way that makes sense to the parish, and stated in a way that is understandable for them. What is taught, then, is not chapter 5 of INVITATION, or chapter 12 of *Catholicism Today*, but rather the faith of this community—and if you want to read more about it, it is also discussed in chapter 5 of this book or chapter 12 of that book.

(2) Another way to develop a curriculum for the catechumenate is to follow the lectionary. The lectionary was designed to give training in the Christian life for adults in the Church. If the catechetical sessions for the catechumenate are held in direct conjunction with the sessions after dismissal, then what is taught should especially follow directly from the readings of the day.

To some people, using the lectionary means that they follow the weekly readings, teaching what flows naturally from it. What is essential in our faith will flow naturally from the lectionary at some point or another. In such cases, it may be necessary to schedule an extra meeting to cover a topic that appears to be neglected, or to delve further into a topic that has not been adequately discussed.

For other people, using the lectionary means developing a curriculum, and then organizing it around the lectionary, rather than around a unit plan or some other unifying principle.

However the curriculum is designed, what is taught should always be connected to the message and experience of Sunday worship, and the dismissal sharing that was part of it.

Models For Catechumenate

Each of the models in this chapter has "worked" in parishes—that is, all have been judged as good by the participants and leaders from their parishes. Each has also been improved and changed from what appears here, and each will continue to be improved and changed for different groups, and using different gifts. Take from these models the ideas you feel will work for you, and adjust them as necessary for your situation; use these ideas to jostle your creativity to come up with better ideas.

Composite Model

A highlight of the Composite Model is the curriculum design for catechetical sessions that is included. While it takes the largest number of pages, notice that it is only one aspect of the model. Later we present other aspects which have equal importance: liturgical celebrations, parish life, broader Church membership, and spiritual direction. It also assumes dismissal with faith sharing each Sunday, with an additional meeting scheduled each week for catechesis.

A title, purpose, and major points are included for each session, along with ideas for some appropriate activities. The best aspect of this model is the attention it gives to comprehensive catechesis, with all its elements. Its weakness is the ease with which it could become simply a good program with little or no attention to the process of conversion happening for each catechumen.

St. Augustine Parish Model

This parish model for catechumenate follows directly on the way the parish does precatechumenate. The participants already have a strong foundation in Scripture behind them. They combine catechesis with dismissal sharing, and find their on-going formation in the lectionary of the Church. This becomes a solid foundation for the future life as a Catholic. Another especially good aspect of this model is the real expectation of regular service on the part of catechumens during this time.

St. Brigid Parish Model

This model highlights one part of the total catechumenate process in the parish. Dismissal is the most significant experience for catechumens, and the RCIA coordinator in the parish has developed extensive materials to help sponsors feel comfortable in the leadership role he calls them to. The materials given show many of the possibilities for beginning dismissal sharing with a group. His caution is important: "There is no need to answer all the questions or puzzle over a question you don't understand. Sharing your feelings on the subject is what is important."

Probably, such extensive materials are not needed as a group becomes more at ease with one another and sponsors get a better feeling of their role. However, if your group has a hard time getting started, an idea like this may be what you need.

COMPOSITE MODEL: CATECHUMENATE

Liturgical Celebrations
Rite of becoming a catechumen—September
Dismissal each Sunday
Blessing—October
Giving a Christian name—November
Exorcism—January

Parish Life
- Sponsors have special responsibility to invite catechumens to parish activities, and to introduce them to appropriate groups and persons within the parish.

- Catechumens make and deliver Christmas baskets, and are expected to volunteer for at least one other service action.
- Catechumens begin using envelopes, and exercising regular stewardship in the parish.
- Choir and music minister teach frequently used hymns in special session with catechumens.

Broader Church Membership
- Tours of local churches of special historical significance.
- Tour National Shrine in Washington.
- Combine with other parishes for specialized events, such as a talk on black Catholic history, and a film on the Old Testament.
- Rite of blessing celebrated with the bishop, with other parishes from the diocese.
- Begin receiving diocesan newspaper.

Spiritual Direction
- Reflection on the Word following dismissal.
- Sponsors responsible for searching out growth and facilitating personal storytelling.
- Interview with parish priest in context of teaching on conscience and confession.
- Interview before the rite of election with catechumenate director.
- Responsibility for taking part in prayer with the group.

Meetings
(see following sheets for outlines)

**Composite Model: Catechumenate Sessions
Session #1: Who Is God?**

Purpose
To reflect together on our experience of God's self-revelation to us; to discuss our faith in the Trinity, and grow in awareness of God as Creator, Son and Spirit.

Major Points
- What can we say about God?
- How have we already learned about God?
- What we know of God we know because God has revealed it to us.
- God wants us to know him.
- Jesus is the Word of God, uniting all revelation.
- The Spirit is their love, their unity, shared with us.
- What meaning can the Trinity have for us?
- The sign of the cross is a basic prayer, and expresses our faith in the Trinity.

Reference: *Invitation*, McBride, Chapter 1 and 2
Illustrated Catechism, Liguori Publications,
Chapter 1, 5, 6.

Session #2: Seeing the Bible as Our Book

Purpose
To introduce the Bible in such a way that it can be used
with some confidence.

Major points
- With the basic divisions of Old and New Testaments,
  the Bible tells the story of how God has dealt with people throughout history.
- It is the story of salvation—God's people continually in
  need of salvation, and God continually saving them.
- Jesus is central; the Old Testament tells how God prepared the world for his coming; the New Testament
  tells about his ministry and its effect.
- The Bible is the inspired Word of God—inspired people passed on their experiences of God, inspired people kept and treasured their stories, the translators
  were inspired, the copiers, and, finally, we are inspired as we read God's Word, and open our hearts to
  it.
- Interpretation depends on prayer and basic knowledge
  of what the author is trying to communicate about God.
- Look at the broad timeline of the Bible, and its major
  points.
- Encourage people to look through the Old Testament
  over the week, and refresh their minds on some of the
  stories they have heard. Give out references for some
  familiar ones.

Reference: *Invitation*, McBride, Chapter 2, 5
Illustrated Catechism, Liguori Pub., Part 1,
#6,7,8
In-depth: *Reading the Old Testament, An In-
troduction,* Boadt.

Suggestion for method
Begin a time line that will teach on a variety of levels:

1. It will visualize the inter-relatedness of Church and
   Scripture. You cannot understand one without the
   other.
2. Filling in a time line as a group allows the members
   to feel good about what they already know. Even if
   they don't know the approximate date, they will know
   some names, events, stories that belong somewhere
   on the time line.
3. The time line includes local experience. It places your

parish, your diocese, and today's questions in the context of the universal Church experience.
4. The time line continues into the future. (What
   changes do you think will happen in the Church?
   When will they occur?) It can prepare people for
   change, and also call for a discussion of personal responsibility in the Church, how to effect change, and
   realistic expectation about change.

In the first session on Scripture, list major dates in
the preparation of Scripture:
1800 (Abraham), 1200 (desert experience, formation of
stories), 900 (David, much of the writing done), 587 (Bab-
ylonian captivity), 300 (Alexander the Great, Septuagint
translation of Scripture), 0 (approximate birth of Christ),
220 (canon of New Testament definite, referred to as New
Testament), 400 (Vulgate translation of whole Bible),
1450 (printing press, Bible printed), 1940 (Dead Sea
scrolls), 1965 (Ebla fragments discovered), 1970 (New
American Translation of Scripture).

In the next session, add more dates, names and significant events. (i.e., Exodus, building the temple,
prophets, situate the Old Testament readings from current Sundays).

The third session on Scripture, add dates for epistles
and gospels, and when they were accepted generally.

As you continue with sessions on the development
of the Church, mark major events and periods in Church
history on the time line. Add the names of well known
saints, some other significant world events, and some lo-
cally important dates. Encourage discussion of the future, marking some significant happenings that the
people would expect, and some idea of when they might
happen.

This visual aid can be left in sight throughout the catechumenate, and may frequently be useful. The stories
of the saints should take on extra meaning if they can be
placed in the context of their Church and world on the
time line; the development of sacraments should make
sense more quickly with this as a background.

Session #3: Tracing Themes through Scripture

Purpose
To show the unity of the Word of God, and to exemplify
how the fullness of meaning comes in Jesus.

Major Points
- A major way to understand and interpret Scripture is
  to see the themes that it develops. As an example, trace
  the names used for God throughout Scripture, and
  show the significance each name had.
- Trace the special theme of covenant/promise.

- Point out other themes people see through Scripture—call and response, prophecy, sin and salvation.

Reference: *Invitation*, McBride, Chap. 2, 4.
Illustrated Catechism, Liguori Pub., Part 1, #6, 7, 8.

Session #4: Using the New Testament

Purpose

To present the New Testament as a gift to us from the early Church; to understand what is included in the New Testament and how to use it.

Major Points
- Jesus's respect for and use of the Scriptures.
- Early Church was action filled, not a writing Church; oral tradition in the New Testament.
- How and why gospels were written; see uniqueness of each one.
- Significance of accepting all four gospels; including Catholic epistles; including an apocalyptic book; what it meant to call this the "New Testament".

Reference: *Invitation*, McBride, Chap. 5, 7, 8.
Illustrated Catechism, Liguori Pub., Part 2, #19, 20.
In-depth resource: *The New Testament, An Introduction*, Perrin and Duling.

Session #5: The Beginning of the Church

Purpose

To give an awareness of what the Church was like in the beginning, forming the foundation for the development of the Church as a worshiping, teaching community.

Major Points
- Small group study on sections of Acts of the Apostles and epistles, looking for what the Church experience was like.
- Point out what was there: the kerygma, authority, Eucharist, ministries, charisms, community, Holy Spirit, diversity.
- Point out what was not there: church buildings, structured roles, etc.

Reference: *Invitation*, McBride, Chap. 8, 9, 10.
Illustrated Catechism, Liguori Pub., Part 2, #18, 19, 21.

Session #6: The Church as Worshiping Community

Purpose

To give an awareness of the worshiping ministry of the Church, and how it has been fulfilled throughout its history.

Major Points
- Our primary act of worship in the Church is the Mass, which is rooted in the Last Supper.
- Point out the similarity between the Mass and the Passover Meal.
- Look at New Testament witness to Eucharist.
- Show historical emphasis on Jesus's divinity: distance of altar, communion bread, experience of simply "attending" Mass; devotions to Mary and saints as a reaction.
- Church reacts with reminders of Jesus's humanity: devotions to stations, nativity sets, and Sacred Heart.
- Effects of Reformation on the Mass: emphasis on structure and ritual.
- Vatican II directs the spirit of the Mass today.
- Look to the future, and prepare catechumens for the variety they will find in the Church.

Reference: *Invitation*, McBride, Chap. 14.
Illustrated Catechism, Liguori Pub., Part 3, #33–38.

Session #7: The Church as Teaching Community

Purpose

To give a sense of the teaching mission of the Church, and how it has been fulfilled throughout history.

Major Points
- Kernel of the teaching structure found in the New Testament: ecumenical councils, primacy of pope, role of bishop.
- Teaching structure today, and how it has developed.
- Role of the laity; discuss other offices in local and universal Church.
- Infallibility and collegiality.
- Introduce the documents of Vatican II and the new Code of Canon Law, and point out some significant passages.
- Look to the future, and discuss how changes come about.

Reference: *Invitation*, McBride, Chap. 11, 18.
Illustrated Catechism, Liguori Pub., Part 2, #24, 25, 26.

Session #8: Mary and the Saints
(schedule at an appropriate time)—This session is good preparation for the rite of giving a Christian name. Sponsors can play an important role in suggesting a particular patron saint that is appropriate to individual catechumens.

Purpose
To point out the role played by Mary in the Catholic Church; to introduce the lives of some of the saints, and to suggest ways that the saints can help us in our lives in the Lord.

Major Points
- The importance of Mary's role; statements of the Church on the value of devotion to Mary.
- Examples of healthy devotion to Mary and saints.
- Highlight some saints with special significance for the catechumens.
- Discuss value of a patron saint; make decision regarding taking a Christian name.

Reference: *Invitation*, McBride, Chap. 22;
Illustrated Catechism, Liguori Pub., Part 4, #76–79.

Session #9: Liturgical Year
(schedule at an appropriate time)

Purpose
To see the liturgical cycles of the Church as a whole, and discuss how they are designed to promote on-going growth experiences for Catholics.

Major Points
- Look at the whole liturgical year cycle.
- Center on present season of the liturgical year.
- Discuss ways of celebrating that particular season.
- Present other cycles happening in the Church: cycle of the saints, the Prayer of Christians, weekly cycles, cycles of lectionary readings at Mass.
- Make suggestions as to personal practices recommended for the various liturgical cycles.

Reference: *Invitation*, McBride, Chap. 23;
Illustrated Catechism, Liguori Pub., Part 5, #88.

Session #10: Jesse Tree
(schedule during Advent)

Purpose
To review Old Testament salvation history; to suggest a practical way to share faith experiences with family members; to celebrate Advent.

Major Points
- Explain the idea of a Jesse Tree.
- Have each person in the group make a symbol for the tree and explain it to the group.

Reference: *Invitation*, McBride, Chap. 6, 23.

Session #11: Jesus at Christmas
(schedule in Advent)

Purpose
To reflect on the significance of the incarnation, the meaning of Christmas, and what we can learn of who Jesus really is.

Major Points
- Study the Christmas story from each gospel and see how it is reflective of the whole gospel's spirit.
- Recall discussion of who God is, and of sin and salvation.
- Discuss the role of Jesus, and the significance of Christmas in the whole of salvation history.
- Share some appropriate ways of celebrating Christmas in the spirit of knowing who Jesus really is—alternate Christmas programs, religious Christmas cards, nativity sets, etc.

Reference: *Invitation*, McBride, Chap. 7;
Illustrated Catechism, Liguori Pub., Part 1, #2, 3, 9, 10.
In-depth: *An Adult Christ at Christmas*, Brown.

Session #12: Sacraments in the Church

Purpose
To describe the seven sacraments so catechumens can identify them, see how they are related to one another, and understand what role they play in the life of a Catholic.

Major Points
- Identify and describe the seven sacraments, and see what groupings exist among them.
- Describe what makes something a sacrament: individual decisions, Church's symbol language and ceremony, and God's action.

- Focus on Eucharist as the central sacrament.

Reference: *Invitation*, McBride, Chap. 12, 14.
           Illustrated Catechism, Liguori Pub., Part 2,
           #23, Part 3, #27
           In-depth: *A New Look at the Sacraments*,
           Bausch.

Suggestions about Methods

Accept the challenge to teach sacrament in such a way that the catechumen understands what Catholics believe about sacraments, but not everything that a person "ought" to experience in sacrament. For instance:

For Baptism, reflect together on the meaning and experience of conversion; talk about water and oil; read the blessing of the baptismal water. Talk about infant Baptism, and the permanence of Baptism. But wait for mystagogia to talk about feeling death and new life, refreshment, strengthening, sweet fragrance, new garment, and loving community.

For Eucharist, reflect together on presence, and presence for a purpose, on our bodies and our selves, on food and the special significance of bread and wine. Make bread, and share it in an intentional community way. Describe the faith of Catholics that recognizes Jesus truly present in Eucharist, and the expressions of that faith in 40 Hours, Benediction, and other Eucharistic Devotions. But wait for mystagogia to taste—then be able to tell the goodness of the Lord; wait to talk about the love relationship expressed and developing; wait to get ready for the daily and ordinary experience of Eucharist.

Sacramental catechesis in catechumenate is like preparation for raising children before you have your own or talking about living in community before you become a member of one. It can be helpful, but it is very different from the sacramental catechesis that can happen in mystagogia. That is like parents sharing experiences of their children or vowed community members meeting to achieve discernment. The experience makes all the difference.

Session #13: Sacraments of Initiation

Purpose
To study the sacraments of initiation in the Church, and Holy Orders.

Major Points
- Baptism and Confirmation are formal expressions of a person's decision to convert, to change his/her life as needed to lead it in the direction of Jesus.

- Through the signs of water, oil, and laying on hands, God shares his own life with us, and gives us what we need to live that life.
- In receiving these sacraments, we also choose ministering membership in the Catholic Church.
- First Eucharist completes our initiation into the Church.
- In Holy Orders, and in priesthood, the call to service and Church membership is focused in a call to serve as leader of the priestly people of God.

Reference: *Invitation*, McBride, Chap. 13, 18.
           Illustrated Catechism, Liguori Pub., Part 3,
           #28–32; 39–41.

Session #14: An Adult Christian Conscience

Purpose
To understand how our conscience works, and how to recognize sin in our life.

Major Points
- Stages of conscience development: instinctive, moral, and religious.
- Role of laws and rules.
- Sin as process; an act of conscience.
- Identifying sin leads us to the need for the Sacrament of Reconciliation.
- Social teaching of the Church (encyclicals, pastoral letters, etc.); reality of social sin.
- Process for conscience decisions.

Reference: *Invitation*, McBride, Chap. 2, 20.
           Illustrated Catechism, Liguori Pub., Part 3,
           #49–63.
           In-depth: *Renewing the Earth: Catholic Documents on Peace, Justice, and Liberation*, O'Brien, ed.

Session #15: Sacrament of Reconciliation

Purpose
To see the Sacrament of Reconciliation as our way of repentance, and coming back to the community.

Major Points
- What we mean by the Sacrament of Reconciliation: what it looks like, how people receive it.
- Reconciliation is the sacramental way of receiving God's forgiveness.

- We hear the words of forgiveness; we should feel the laying on of hands which is a natural, human way for people to receive peace and forgiveness.
- We are also re-united with the community, whose forgiveness we also need because of our sin.
- How will catechumens experience their first confession, and how will they prepare for it?
- How do they feel about it?

Reference: *Invitation*, McBride, Chap. 15.
               Illustrated Catechism, Liguori Pub., Part 3, #48, 64–68.

Session #16: Sacrament of Marriage

Purpose
To see Marriage as a sacrament, with implications for the whole Church, as well as the couple.

Major Points
- Sacramental aspects of marriage: decision, symbol, God's action.
- Planning for marriage.
- The Sacrament of Marriage for the already married catechumen.
- Church law and marriage.
- Discuss questions of annulments and divorce and the Catholic Church.

References: *Invitation*, McBride, Chap. 17.
            Illustrated Catechism, Liguori Pub., Part 3, #42–46.
            Specialized: *Annulments: Your Chance to Remarry in the Catholic Church*, Cwack.

Session #17: The Family as Domestic Church

Purpose
To highlight the dignity of the family, and to consider the effects faith and conversion have on the family.

Major Points
- Family as basic social unit.
- God is love; God's presence, in love, in every family.
- Sharing faith in your family—helps and hindrances.
- When your marriage becomes "a mixed marriage"; dealing with religious differences in a family.

Reference: *Invitation*, McBride, Chap. 17.
            Illustrated Catechism, Liguori Pub., Part 3, #47.

Session #18: Eucharist

Purpose
To look again at Eucharist as a sacrament, and to reflect on its meaning and centrality in our faith.

Major Points
- Meaning of real presence.
- Implications of our faith in the real presence.
- Our practices regarding Eucharist.
- Eucharist in the midst of the sacraments, and our faith life.
- Appreciating other modes of presence: in the Word, in the poor, in community.
- Symbolism of bread and wine.

Reference: *Invitation*, McBride, Chap. 14.

OTHER MODELS
**The Catechumenate Period
at Saint Augustine Parish (1982)
Catechumenate Director: John Butler**

The basic elements of the catechumenate period at our parish are:

1. Dismissal occurs each Sunday; catechumens meet for an hour and a half in reflection on Scripture and catechesis.

2. Sponsors are in place at this point and are encouraged to be fellow journeyers throughout this process.

3. Each catechumen is expected to make a decision for some specific on-going service with the parish, giving at least two hours a week. Sponsors are a particular help in this choice, as well as the information previously received during the precatechumenate from parish leaders.

4. Each catechumen receives envelopes.

5. Major catechesis is developed during this period, with specific connections to the gospel readings from each Sunday. We have no fixed agenda of topics as such, but react to the specific needs of the group each year. There is care, however, that the major teachings of the Church are included for each group.

Each week, at least 20 minutes is given to specific reflection on the gospel, with the focus "What am I being challenged to, by these words?" Sometimes, a lecture is given, on a topic such as the prophets, women in the Old Testament, or black theology, liberation theology, etc. Usually there is small group sharing around the gospel, or another topic for the day. Reflection on other areas of Scripture are included, with presentation of themes.

Care is given to integrate what they are doing in parish ministry with the gospel. Sacraments, structure, authority—all the teachings of the Church—are presented before Lent begins, with an emphasis on their roots in Scripture.

The period ends with a major interview or discernment period. This one is with the catechumen and the sponsor, the director and the catechist. The sponsor should be perceived as a partner to the catechumen in this interview, and care must be taken that the candidate doesn't feel overwhelmed by the number of people involved. The purpose of this interview is to discover the true motives and intentions behind the catechumen's desire to be initiated. Often, the original motive may have been the attraction of the gospel choir, or family pressure; at this point, we seek a real desire to be part of the Catholic Church. An important question asked is "If this parish were to cease to exist, would you still want to become a Catholic?"

What we are trying to discern is conversion; initial conversion might have occurred before the catechumenate; what has happened during the course of the catechumenate? What has changed? What movement can be seen? Usually, there are clear statements of change at this point.

Sometimes, as a result of their responses, or because of their lack of regularity in participation, we ask catechumens to give themselves more time with the process and not seek election. Usually we do this by pushing a question or point, helping them see their unreadiness.

Sometimes, we simply must say no. Their reaction to this may change our minds; but we must retain the right to refuse initiation, if the process is to be meaningful. It is a difficult decision. We certainly feel inadequate to judge someone in this regard. However, we have an obligation to discern conversion and proper motive, or we are simply churning out new members.

This period of the catechumenate ends with the celebration of election on the first Sunday of Lent. We celebrate in our parish, and then join with other parishes for the rite with the bishop at the cathedral.

Catechumenate Period
St. Brigid Parish, Hanford, California
Catechumenate Director: Larry Shehan

Dismissal sessions are a key element in the catechumenate period. The director at this parish has prepared support sheets for sponsors in his parish, so that they feel more comfortable leading these sessions. This is a sample of those guide sheets, one prepared for the third Sunday of Advent, Cycle A

Directions: Break up into groups of four members each, two candidates with their sponsors. Choose a different pair each week. Each group will be at a table numbered #1, #2 or #3. These numbers stand for first, second or third reading, and will tell you which reading to begin your discussion with.

Recall the reading you are to begin with. (You may wish to read it over again together, or to refer to the commentary sheet provided for you.)

Now discuss the questions for the reading listed below. There is no need to answer all the questions or puzzle over a question you don't understand. Sharing your feelings on the subject is what is important. Now it's up to you. Go to it!

Questions relating to first reading: (Is. 35:1–6,10)

1. Am I in the desert, the parched land? How? What hope is given to me?

2. Are my hands feeble? How does God strengthen them? Are my knees weak? How does God make them firm?

3. Is my heart frightened? Do I hope?

4. Is he my springtime when all I see is winter? (What does that mean?)

5. In what ways am I blind, deaf, lame, dumb?

Questions relating to second reading: (Jas. 5:7–10)

1. Why does St. James advise patience especially for those beginning their journey of faith?

2. Why is impatience about your journey a danger to be avoided?

3. Why does the farmer need patience? How does his situation apply to me?

4. Why is patience with yourself so important?

5. We must wait patiently for God's will and God's time. What does that mean in practical terms?

Questions relating to gospel reading: (Mt. 11:2–11)

1. John asks for certainty. In answer, Jesus asks for faith. How does this apply to us?

2. What proofs does Jesus send to John that he is the Messiah? Are these proofs for you? What do they mean?

3. Why am I in the desert? Did I just go out to *see*, or did I go out to *do* (to cross the desert and climb the mountain)?

4. Can we successfully cross the desert and climb the mountain *alone?* What does that mean for you?

PARISH WORKSHEET

1. How will you design your catechumenate period?

2. How will you facilitate the spirit of community within the group?

3. Who will be the primary catechist?

4. What will be your curriculum?

5. What materials are needed for catechists and for participants?

6. How will you assure a variety of adult learning methods?

7. How will you evaluate the presentations?

8. How will participants be welcomed into parish life?

9. Who will follow up on commitments to service?

10. What tours or additional experiences will be planned?

11. Who will pay special attention to the spiritual growth of catechumens?

12. Will you call for regular use of a journal, or other written reflection?

13. Who will do the interview that helps individuals and the parish decide as to readiness for the rite of election?

14. On what basis will this decision be made?

Chapter VI

The RCIA Experience: Enlightenment/Purification

- ■ Introducing the Period
- ■ What the Document Says
- ■ Meet the Elect
- ■ Significant Issues in Enlightenment/Purification
- ■ Composite Model
- ■ Other Models
- ■ Parish Worksheet

INTRODUCING THE PERIOD: ENLIGHTENMENT/PURIFICATION

Enlightenment/Purification: A time of spiritual reflection in preparation for the celebration of Easter and Initiation. The period coincides with the season of Lent, the formal time of renewal within the Church. Lent should be understood as the time for the Church to prepare for the new life of Easter that comes with the initiation of new members.

The Triduum is the special sacred time that ends Lent and begins the Easter celebration. It begins Holy Thursday evening, and continues through Easter Sunday. While it is not specifically a part of RCIA, those holy days are the heart of the entire Christian year, and should hold that significance for the elect and the RCIA team.

Guidelines for the Purification/Enlightenment Period:

1. This is a time for spiritual formation, not catechesis.

2. It should provide opportunities to try new forms of prayer and challenges to further growth in prayer.

3. The purification/enlightenment period for the elect should be a focal point for the parish experience of Lent.

4. The daily and the Sunday lectionary contain especially appropriate material for reflection during the period.

Time Frame: Lent

Liturgical Celebrations:
   Election (RCIA #106–137 and 530–561)—first Sunday of Lent
   Scrutinies (RCIA #141–146; 151–156; 164–177)—third, fourth, and fifth Sundays of Lent
   Presentations (RCIA #147–149; 157–163; 178–184)
   Preparatory rites (RCIA #185–205)—Holy Saturday morning
   Initiation (RCIA #208–234)—Easter Vigil

To learn more about this period, see:

Boyack, *A Parish Guide*, Chap. 4.

Dunning, *New Wine, New Wineskins*, Chap. 5.

Gusmer, "Lent, Community Conversion", *C.I.R. I*, Enlightenment G.

Hovda, "Lent in the Parish", *C.I.R. II*, Enlightenment H.

Kemp, *Journey in Faith*, Chap. 4.

RCIA, Introduction, #118–128; 138–140.

WHAT THE DOCUMENT SAYS ABOUT ENLIGHTENMENT/PURIFICATION

#4 & 5   The whole community is involved in and benefits from the RCIA. The RCIA responds to individual spiritual journeys and is flexible enough to meet individual needs.

#121   The rite of election is the turning point of the whole RCIA.

#119   The rite of election signals admission to the next celebration of the sacraments of initiation. This admission by the Church is founded in election by God, in whose name the Church acts.

#11   The godparent is chosen by the Church, and becomes official and permanent at the rite of election.

#6.2   After the rite of election, there is to be a more profound preparation for the sacraments.

#7.3   The period happens during Lent, and should include purification and enlightenment (illumination).

#8   Lent achieves its full force in the community when it is focused on a profound preparation of the elect.

#9.4   During Lent the faithful should give good example to the elect by participating in the rites and by their own renewal in the spirit of penance, faith and charity.

#138   In its liturgy, and in its liturgical catechesis, Lent is a memorial of or a preparation for Baptism, and a time of penance. Lent renews the community as well as the elect, as they prepare to celebrate the paschal mystery.

#138   Catechumens and the local community are called to spiritual recollection during Lent.

#139   The method is to be spiritual recollection rather than catechesis. It is to be accomplished primarily through the celebration of rites.

#139   The preparation of the elect is completed through the rites.

#141   The three scrutinies are celebrated to reveal whatever is weak or sinful so it may be healed, and whatever is upright and holy so it may be strengthened.

#141   The scrutinies are to purify, strengthen, and make firm the catechumens in their journey to God. They achieve this mainly through the exorcisms.

#142   Scrutinies help the elect progress in sincere self-knowledge, serious appraisal of self, and true penance.

#145   The scrutinies are to be celebrated in the community by a priest or deacon so that the faithful can also benefit from them.

#20   The scrutinies are very important, and should not be neglected except for serious reason.
The period of enlightenment should not last more than eight weeks.

#147   Presenting the creed and the Lord's Prayer to the elect is to enlighten them particularly in preparation for their participation in Mass.

#185   Holy Saturday completes the period. On this day, it is appropriate to gather the elect for preparation rites. It should be a day set apart from ordinary life as far as possible, calling the elect and those ministering to them to refrain from ordinary work and fast if possible.

MEET THE ELECT

As team members help the elect through this period of final preparation for initiation, they witness the flowering of the conversion experience. Concentration is focused on God, and the ways God is present to this person. Strong challenges, great hope, deep faith and peace are usually evident. Statements like these can be expected:

"I feel as though I am on the top of a mountain. I never want to leave it."

"I never told you this, but there were some things we talked about that didn't really make sense to me. I just let some of them slide. They must have been important, though, because I kept thinking about them. You know what? Now I believe. I really believe."

"I feel as though I have finally come to know the Holy Spirit. I thought I did before, but things are different now."

"God is so full of surprises. I never know what to expect."

"I was wary of the idea of trying new forms of prayer. I felt so comfortable with what I was already doing. I'm glad you pushed us some. There are whole new worlds out there."

SIGNIFICANT ISSUES IN ENLIGHTENMENT/ PURIFICATION

Spiritual Direction

Spiritual direction should begin long before this period, but it should flower and be highlighted during it, as specific attention is paid to spiritual growth and development. In the past, many parish teams looked to professional ministers (usually the priest) to provide all the spiritual direction in the RCIA as well as in other areas of parish life. A more recent trend is recognizing the gifts of spiritual direction found in parishioners.

A primary reason for this is the spiritual hunger that is felt more and more among adults today. Many people who come to adult education programs, most of those who come into the various renewal programs, and certainly everyone who becomes aware of a conversion experience within, feel a need for spiritual direction. They want and need help along their journey to God, in deepening their prayer communication, and their personal relationship with God.

While classical spiritual direction may be the territory of professional ministers, there is a level of spiritual friendship or companionship that can be offered by gifted members of the community. In the RCIA especially, the team has a responsibility to find those parishioners so gifted, and place their gifts at the service of catechumens.

This ministry of spiritual direction is different from the ministry of the sponsor. First of all, it is more specialized. The sponsor shares all aspects of the journey with the catechumen, and should have the experience of growing along with them, while the spiritual friend focuses on the spiritual journey experienced by the catechumen. The sponsor's role is an official one in the Church, and part of their responsibility is to the Church. They are asked to take part in discernment, and occasionally to discuss the progress of the catechumen with others on the team. The spiritual director, on the other hand, has a priviliged relationship that must always be confidential. Nothing shared in that relationship should be discussed with anyone else. Finally, the role of sponsor is one that can be filled by an average good Catholic. Very little specialized training is required. For a spiritual director however, there are some more requirements.

Usually one who has the gifts for spiritual direction is already being asked for spiritual guidance in some ways. She or he would be one others are already asking for advice or counsel on spiritual matters. The persons should certainly be experiencing spiritual direction themselves. A potential spiritual guide needs sufficient time to devote to this personal ministry. Most such gifted people would also be looking for opportunities for workshops in spiritual direction, or at least books or articles that would increase familiarity with the resources for classical spiritual direction.

Experience of Evil, and Exorcism

The celebration of the scrutinies calls us to express what we believe about evil. The scrutinies remind us that evil is a significant force in our lives. Alone, we are powerless before it. Our need for salvation is often difficult for us to acknowledge. We have a basic difficulty accepting the reality of evil. We are used to depending on ourselves as rugged individualists. The scrutinies challenge us to break through all these barriers, acknowledge dependence on God, and our battles against evil.

We are thirsty, as the woman at the well was thirsty, and often ignore Jesus's offer of living water. We are blind in so many ways, as blind as the man born blind; only Jesus can heal us and give us our sight once again. We are dead as surely as Lazarus was dead and buried in the tomb, with the sin that has infected us. Only Jesus can bring us back to life.

Celebrating the scrutinies should affect the whole parish, not just the elect. It should call us with the power of the Lenten experience to see sin in our lives, and to acknowledge our need for God. Each of us benefits from the scrutiny, as we look hard at our lives and see it with the light of the gospel message.

Cycle A Readings

When a parish is involved in RCIA, it is permitted to use the readings of cycle A every year for the Lent and Easter season. They are particularly suited to the celebration of the rites. This is most significant in the readings for the third, fourth, and fifth Sundays of Lent. In cycle A, these are from the gospel of John, the story of the Samaritan woman at the well, the cure of the man born blind, and the raising of Lazarus from the dead. The scrutinies assume these readings in the language and symbolism used.

Some parishes choose instead to use the cycle used by the rest of the Church, and make the necessary adjustments in the rites celebrated. (See sample scrutiny to celebrate with cycle B readings in Chapter VIII of this Manual.) Their reasons center on the desire to remain united with the rest of the Church, and often to use the lectionary services available in the Church, which follow the current cycle.

Whichever decision is made for the local parish, the team must assure that the rites are celebrated meaningfully, and that the RCIA keeps its central position in the Church, especially during Lent.

Models for Enlightenment/Purification

These models show some of the ways that parishes have met the challenges of enlightenment/purification.

All of them include clear attention to personal prayer, and membership in the praying community. What is described here is what happens in addition to the celebration of the rites. Remember that those liturgical actions are to be the center of the period.

Composite Model

The key to this model is that the sessions are primarily times for prayer together. Each meeting involves a presentation about a method of prayer, and then time to experience that kind of prayer. Special care is needed to insure that the time not be spent simply in talking prayer, but in doing prayer.

St. Augustine Parish Model

The description of the model at St. Augustine shows the heavy emphasis placed on celebrating the rites of the RCIA, as well as other liturgical actions in the parish. The introduction of a significant time of retreat shows their appreciation of the work of the Spirit through this time. In more recent years, the parish has expanded the retreat time, and diminished the time for sessions.

St. Joseph Parish Model

The outstanding aspect of this model is the focus on the scrutinies. Involving the elect in their preparation allows the celebrations to be truly personal and powerful. The retreat also leads very directly to the Easter Vigil and relates it to the experience of Eucharist beyond that day.

COMPOSITE MODEL: ENLIGHTENMENT/ PURIFICATION

Liturgical Celebrations
Election: first Sunday of Lent
Scrutinies: third, fourth, fifth Sundays of Lent
Presentation of creed: by Parish Council, on third Sunday of Lent
Claiming of the Lord's Prayer: After session in the fourth week of Lent
Blessing: By family members and friends, after session in the fifth week of Lent.

Parish Life
- The Parish Council invites the elect to a dinner in their honor, at which parish leadership welcomes them, explains the structure of the parish, and invites participation where appropriate.
- Sessions on prayer during Lent are open to total parish participation; several parishioners participate as a Lenten growth activity, and benefit with closer contact with the elect.

Broader Church Awareness
- The rite of election and preparatory rites are celebrated with the bishop and with the elect from other parishes. The Holy Saturday morning gathering includes sharing among the elect.

Spiritual Direction
The total period is dedicated to spiritual growth; discussion of, and participation in varied forms of prayer is the regular experience in weekly sessions. Each participant is challenged to be open to and share growth in the life of the spirit during the meetings.

Social Ministry
- Fasting and almsgiving are encouraged; a group service project is undertaken.

Composite Model: Enlightenment/Purification Sessions

Week of Ash Wednesday: The Meaning of Lent

Purpose
To put the season of Lent into perspective—the individual conversion journey and the community's conversion journey.

Major Points
- Lent is the time for the Church to renew itself as it prepares to celebrate Easter. This season calls us annually to look at ourselves as Church, and come closer to fulfilling our call to be the holy people of God.
- We are called to individual and community prayer, fasting, and almsgiving.
- Encourage a commitment to some specific actions during Lent, talk about them with the group, and make them part of the catechumenate community's Lenten experience.

Related Material: *Invitation*, McBride, Chap. 9, 23.

First Week of Lent: Roots of Prayer

Purpose
To recognize each person's gift of prayer, to celebrate the growth all can perceive in their individual prayer lives, and to focus on the Lord's Prayer as a way of life for those who have accepted Jesus.

Major Points
- Sharing how each participant has experienced and grown in prayer over recent months.

- This is to be perceived in light of a lifelong growth process. What helps are needed to promote this growth?
- The Lord's Prayer puts into words the lifestyle Jesus taught (praise, working for the Kingdom, acceptance of God's will, dependence on God, forgiveness).
- As elect, we have a special right to pray the Lord's Prayer, and we formally claim that in our community.
- Close with a formal time to claim the Lord's Prayer with new understanding and vigor. This formal prayer time is the presentation of the Lord's Prayer for the parish, adapted from RCIA #178–183.

Related Material: *Invitation*, McBride, Chap. 26.

Second Week of Lent: The Prayer Within

Purpose
To challenge the elect to a deeper awareness of meditation and mental prayer, and to encourage such prayer in their lives.

Major Points
- Time set aside regularly for prayer is important.
- Ease with non-verbal prayer shows a development in relationship.
- Techniques and expectations for spiritual reading and reflection, meditation, and contemplation.
- Time for silent prayer before the Blessed Sacrament.

Third Week of Lent: Popular Devotions and Their Role in the Prayer Tradition of the Church

Purpose
To acknowledge and evaluate the extensive devotional tradition within the Catholic Church.

Major Points
- Discuss personal experience or questions regarding devotions.
- Present reasons for development of devotions through history.
- Discuss development of a well-rounded prayer life including some devotions.
- Describe the many facets of the rosary as prayer. Pray the rosary together.

Related Material: *Invitation*, McBride, Chap. 22

Fourth Week of Lent: Sharing Prayer: The Value of Small Groups in Prayer

Purpose
To promote appreciation of shared prayer in small and large groups, particularly in families; to talk about charismatic prayer communities; to encourage a sense of community in our prayer life.

Major Points
- Recall our need for community.
- Share successes and difficulties with family prayer.
- Describe charismatic communities.
- Discuss how to initiate prayer with others.
- Spend some time in shared prayer.

Related Material: *Invitation*, McBride, Chap. 3.

Fifth Week of Lent: The Formal Prayer of the Church

Purpose
To emphasize the centrality of Sunday Eucharist as our formal community prayer, and in particular, the coming celebration of the Triduum.

Major Points
- Regular participation in Sunday Eucharist is key to membership in the Church, and should be central in our personal prayer life.
- Particular local ways to celebrate Sundays. Recalling a sense of the holy that pervaded the experience of Sundays in our grandparents' day. Discussion of appropriate and inappropriate activities for the Lord's Day.
- Discussion of the Triduum and Easter as the basis for all Sundays. Describe how the elect will be involved in those celebrations.

OTHER MODELS
Enlightenment/Purification Period
at Saint Augustine Parish (1982), Washington, D.C.
Catechumenate Director: John Butler

We continue the catechumenal sessions and dismissal, but with a sense of going deeper, and heightened anticipation of initiation.

An outstanding event during this period is a one day Lenten Retreat. (We hope to move to a weekend retreat in the future.) It is a time for deep sharing about where they are spiritually, and an opportunity for real sharing of themselves. It has always resulted in an emotional, deep witness experience for the participants, and a heightened sense of community among the catechumens and sponsors.

We challenge them to attend Mass daily, if possible, and to develop a sense and practice of daily prayer in earnest. Fasting is recommended throughout Lent. We celebrate the scrutinies every year, and use the A cycle of readings for their powerful impact. Of course, we use the teachable moments of Lent, and the whole liturgical year, to express the various elements of our faith.

Holy Week becomes the climax of the whole process. We ask the elect to be present for each day's celebration, and unite their journey with that of the Church.

Those who are candidates for reception into full communion receive reconciliation for the first time, with the rest of the parish at a communal penance service, and the catechumens are asked to attend, but without sacramental participation.

On Good Friday, our parish has Stations of the Cross twice, once inside, and once outside through the neighborhood. The participation of the elect is a chance for public witness during this Holy Week.

On Holy Saturday there is a prayer service at noon followed by a brief rehearsal. The Vigil begins at 10 p.m.; the first two parts of the service, the service of light and the liturgy of the word, are shared in common with the Lutheran church across the street. The congregations alternate hosting the celebration of this first portion of the liturgy. The initiation follows in our church as the highpoint of the Vigil.

Candidates for full communion and catechumens are distinguished throughout the process, but it is particularly clear this night, as those already baptized come in robed in white and the non-baptized enter with their sponsors carrying their white robes, which they will receive after Baptism.

Slides of the group throughout the catechumenate process are used where appropriate during the liturgy of the word, to show the centrality of the elect to this service, and to facilitate meditation.

Groups from previous years are introduced and welcomed in a special way after the initiation. The parish has a breakfast after the Vigil to congratulate the neophytes and to continue the celebration. On Easter Day they return to the 12 Noon Mass, are introduced to the community, and are invited to share with the congregation some reflections on their reception.

Two areas of growth for the future are the movement to Baptism by immersion and the request that the neophytes wear their white robes for the Sundays of Easter.

Enlightenment/Purification Period
St. Joseph Parish, Sykesville, Maryland
Virginia Neimeyer, Catechumenate Director

Enlightenment in our parish has taken its rightful place as a unique period in the journey for catechumens and candidates. We make it clear to all concerned that catechumenate has ended. The schedule of meetings changes, the leader for sessions is different, and the room looks quite different once we pass the first Sunday of Lent.

The Rite of Election forms the bridge to this period. It is a powerful experience of God's call, and after it the elect are ready to let God prepare them for the Easter mysteries. There are three main parts to the Lenten journey: the celebration of the scrutinies, including three evenings of reflection in preparation for them; a day-long retreat in which to enter more deeply into the Paschal Mystery; and Holy Week and Easter itself.

The evenings of reflection help both the team and the elect prepare for the scrutiny. Without describing the rite, we invite the elect to consider the need for healing in their personal lives. We center on a symbol, and with prayer and music, call on those present to discover, in small faith-sharing groups, the specific areas needing healing in their lives.

To prepare for the first scrutiny, we center on a pitcher of water, and ask, "In what ways am I needy, thirsty, hungry? How can almsgiving open me to God's grace?" For the second scrutiny, we focus on a lighted candle, and ask, "How am I blind? What do I refuse to see? What is God revealing to me in prayer?" For the third scrutiny, we center on an empty earthen vessel, and ask, "How do I crowd out the presence of God? Where am I called to fast, to make space for God?"

Each evening's discussion leads to mention of specific areas of sinfulness: materialism, lack of trust, selfishness, laziness. The scrutiny celebrated the following Sunday then mentions those specific kinds of evil, and calls on God's power to change us, to heal us of those very specific evils in our lives. Those evenings of reflection, along with the continuing time for dismissal sharing on Sunday mornings, make the scrutinies the powerful experiences they are supposed to be.

The Lenten retreat calls the whole RCIA family to gather together in a beautiful setting outside our parish. Sponsors, spouses, the team and the elect join for a whole Saturday towards the end of Lent to consider the Paschal Mystery. We see it happening in the springtime of nature that surrounds us; we discover and share ways death and resurrection have been part of our lives and relationships; we describe and prepare for the Triduum which ritualizes the Paschal Mystery; and we hear about the Liturgy of the Eucharist which expresses this mystery of our faith.

The music of the liturgy of the Eucharist forms the skeleton of the day. We begin in praise with "Holy, Holy." We learn to sing the mystery of our faith: "Christ has died, Christ has risen, Christ will come again." By the end of the day, we are ready to sing

"Amen," and mean "Yes. I agree. This is *my* faith." The retreat day is the real preparation for the experience of Holy Week.

Our goal throughout this period is to bring people to a point where they are ready to experience the events of Holy Week with a freshness and openness that allows the celebrations to speak for themselves. We do not practice, review or prepare in the sense that people know what is coming next. (Of course, *some* people practice—sponsors, team members, celebrants, but never the elect.) One is ready simply to live through the liturgies and let God's power flow through them.

PARISH WORKSHEET

1. How will you design your enlightenment/purification period?

2. What prayer experiences will you highlight?

3. Who are the best people to share about how to pray, and lead others to pray?

4. How will the parish be connected to the experience of the elect?

5. How will the centrality of the liturgical celebrations be reflected in the total purification/enlightenment period?

6. How will you arrange for the Sacrament of Reconciliation for those people who are already baptized?

Chapter VII

The RCIA Experience: Mystagogia

- ■ Introducing the Period
- ■ What the Document Says
- ■ Meet the Neophyte
- ■ Significant Issues in Mystagogia
- ■ Composite Model
- ■ Other Models
- ■ Parish Worksheet

INTRODUCING THE PERIOD: MYSTAGOGIA

Mystagogia: Time for reflection on the mysteries of membership in the Church.

Guidelines for the mystagogia period:

1. The immediate period of mystagogia, Easter to Pentecost, is time for the neophytes to unwind and to work out their place in the community, as they now experience that full membership.

2. The educational method switches to that of reflection on experience.

3. There are no liturgical rites presented for the period, but it would be appropriate to design one or more to celebrate during it.

4. Rooting in some on-going parish group is important.

5. This can be an appropriate time for the first experience of the Sacrament of Reconciliation.

6. Sunday Eucharist and the lectionary for this season should be the principal experience of mystagogia.

7. The period calls us to experience our faith as mystery. We understand best when we understand as mystery.

Time Frame: Easter Season (Easter to Pentecost) (In addition, some sort of planned follow-up care is needed beyond this time, *see* National Statutes, #24.)

Liturgical Celebrations:
None specified
Possible diocesan gathering for Eucharist with the bishop
Possible closing celebration in the parish near Pentecost

To learn more about this period, see:

Barbernitz, "Welcome to Mystagogia", *Chicago Catechumenate.*

Boyack, *A Parish Guide*, Chap. 5.

Clay, Michael, "Mystagogia and Catechesis on the Sacraments", *Chicago Catechumenate*, Vol. 6, No. 4.

Dunning, *New Wine, New Wineskins*, Chap. 5.

Ebner, "On Shaping Christians and Renewing Parishes", C.I.R. II, Mystagogia C.

Kemp, *Journey in Faith*, Chap. 5.

Kemp, "Mystagogia: A Time to be Fully Alive", C.I.R. II, Mystagogia D.

WHAT THE DOCUMENT SAYS ABOUT MYSTAGOGIA

#4 and #5 The whole community is involved in and benefits from the RCIA. The RCIA responds to individual spiritual journeys and is flexible enough to meet individual needs.

#7.4 Mystagogia happens during the Easter season. It is also called postbaptismal catechesis. It is a time for fuller experiences, for deepening, increasing. It is marked by new experiences of the sacraments and the Christian community.

#244 The community and the neophytes are to experience this period together. It includes meditating on the gospels, experiencing Eucharist, and works of charity; its goal is a fuller experience of the paschal mystery.

#245 The focus of the period is a fuller understanding of our faith as mystery. The experience of receiving the sacraments and participating in the community of the faithful open the way to this new level of understanding.

#246 The relationship between the neophyte and the community is formalized during this period, as new members take their proper position in the community. The community itself benefits with renewed vision and new impetus.

#247 The main place for mystagogia is Sunday Eucharist. Cycle A readings are particularly appropriate, and may always be used.

#25 Joint participation in the Masses of the Easter Season is of great importance for neophytes and for the community.

#248 They should keep their special places in the assembly during this period, and should be mentioned in the homily and the general intercessions.

#246 A major focus of the period should be full and joyful rooting in the community.

#249 It is appropriate to hold some closing celebration on or around Pentecost to complete the RCIA experience.

#251 It is also appropriate that the newly baptized gather to celebrate Eucharist with the bishop during this period.

#250 A possible way to continue some on-going contact and support with new members is to celebrate the anniversary of Baptism each year.

MEET THE NEOPHYTE

Ministers in this final period of the RCIA have two challenges unique to the period. The first is that many of their feelings and statements may be quite similar to those of the neophytes. A great level of sharing will have developed, and the experience of coming to closure and moving on are much the same for both the ministers and the neophytes. The second challenge is the fact that those same ministers should now be involved with new people who are into evangelization and precatechumenate.

These statements reflect some of the spirit of mystagogia.

"Why isn't everybody in the Church as excited as I am?"

"Why can't I volunteer for all those things next year?"

"Let's keep on meeting!"

"Can I come back again next year?"

"I feel kind of lost. So much has happened. I waited so long for this, and now it's over."

"I thought I understood all of this, and now I discover I have even more questions."

"Now what?"

SIGNIFICANT ISSUES IN MYSTAGOGIA

Ministry

Membership in the Church must be ministering membership. One of the emphases that has re-appeared in the Church because of the RCIA is the recognition of the meaning of adult membership. It must mean a membership that feels ownership, and acts with responsibility. It must be a membership that takes ministry seriously.

Ministry should begin during the catechumenate.

Catechumens are to be challenged to service, experiencing the fact that every follower of Christ is called to serve. They should have come to know the variety of ways the parish is involved in service, so that by the time they reach mystagogia, they are ready to make a more informed decision about the ministry they are called to in the Church.

Ministry must be understood in its fullest sense. Special caution should be taken that it not be identified only with "Church work". There are three general areas of ministry with special significance for neophytes:

1. *Evangelization:* Every neophyte has a special charism for evangelization. The experience of first coming to faith is a special gift from which most parishioners are far removed. Those among us who are close to that time, to "the hour I first believed", have a unique opportunity to spread the enthusiasm and excitement of believing in Jesus. Every neophyte is called to evangelize in some way.

2. *Ministry outside the Church:* Neophytes continue living in the same neighborhoods, with the same family, working in the same job, but now they are different. They should experience the call to be ministers in the world in a very real way. The call to all the laity is to be ministers *in* the world, not out of the world.

This is realized best when neophytes are encouraged to identify those areas of their daily lives where they are called to act out of their Christian commitment. Where do they meet the poor or sick or lonely, and find in them the face of Jesus? What decisions face them at work or in neighborhood situations where the Christian response is counter to the common response? What family responsibilities do they carry that call them to generosity, prayer, and sacrifice? How will they bring Christ to the world in which they live, and bring the world in which they live to Christ?

3. *Ministry within the Church community:* An important part of the new member's experience of really belonging is the role they play within parish structures. It is especially important that they become part of an ongoing group that can provide them with some experiences of community, outside of the worshiping community on Sunday. Usually, this will be a work group or committee within the parish structure. Activities like fund raising, planning committees, and maintenance work are valid ways for the neophytes to express their commitment to the Church. Sponsors and team members should assist the neophyte in choosing appropriate activities within the parish.

Some ministries are usually not appropriate for a new member, e.g., parish council president, CCD teacher, RCIA sponsor. Such roles require more experience. Others are particularly appropriate for new members: membership on planning committees that need new ideas; helpers and witnesses in sacrament preparation programs, especially for teenagers and other adults; greeters at liturgies.

On-Going Care; Ending the RCIA

What happens at the end of mystagogia? There are really two issues to consider in answering that question. First, neophytes do need some on-going care. Even the name neophyte—"newly planted"—indicates the need for nurture and on-going care. Regardless of how well the neophytes have been initiated into the community, they are new members, and they need some kind of on-going help.

The other side of the question is that the person is now a member. Sooner or later, the special care must end, and the person is treated as a member like everyone else. The RCIA does not go on forever. It is over with the feast of Pentecost and the end of mystagogia. The National Statutes for the U.S. do recommend a monthly gathering for neophytes to help in this transition (#24). Each neophyte has the responsibility for finding a community of on-going support where the focus is not self-nurture, but working for the kingdom.

Some ideas for appropriate on-going care:

An anniversary celebration of initiation should be held each year. The idea of a reunion can be a reason to contact those who may have drifted away over the year, and a good way to rekindle the faith.

The relationship with a sponsor is supposed to be an on-going relationship that lasts throughout the person's life. The spiritual guide or director who was part of the RCIA experience should also continue for as long as the partners deem necessary, and when they end their relationship, it hopefully means the new member is moving on to a new spiritual director. These special friendships form the kernel of the network of communities that support the developing life of faith for us all.

Some ideas to end the RCIA appropriately:

Neophytes should ordinarily not become volunteers for future groups. Even though they have much experience to share with new catechumens, their connection to the process would encourage holding on to the community of nurture, rather than adult participation in the community.

The monthly gatherings for follow-up with neophytes during the year should be helping them move beyond membership in that community. Some groups will want to keep tighter hold on the group—to "go on meeting." Those that do should have the responsibility to do that without help from outside. Of course, if some people want to meet, the parish cannot stop them. But we can leave the responsibility for that to them, and help them with other relationships in the same way we would if they were not meeting. Almost always, these groups do not go on for long. People do get involved in other areas of parish life, and the fact is that the people really are ready to move on to other things.

Models For Mystagogia

Programming for the mystagogia period has often been perceived by teams as the most difficult. The problem often results in a lack of preparation by the team, or in a lack of participation on the part of neophytes. The three models described here show plans made well ahead of time. As with all good planning for the RCIA, the plans must be flexible, created anew each year, and responsive to particular needs and gifts within a group.

Composite Model

The best aspect of this model is the solid content appropriate for mystagogia that is presented. It can be a real help in dealing with what is still needed in mystagogia after good catechesis in the catechumenate. There is something needed, and it is something that cannot be done without the experience the neophyte has had. There are at least two cautions as you consider this model: Mystagogia must not feel like the periods of catechumenate or enlightenment. This is a danger when the structure of sessions remains the same. Secondly, while there is some benefit to including an experience of reconciliation during this period, it may well be too early in the Christian life for that.

St. Augustine Parish Model

This model is less formal. The meetings on Sunday re-enforce the centrality of Sunday Eucharist to the experience of mystagogia. Discussion is clearly responsive to the neophytes' current and past experience. The best aspect of this model is the demonstrated way in which the new Catholic's on-going life in the Church is based on living out the Sunday worship experience. Its weakest aspect is its informality. It is too easy to confuse informality with unimportance.

Our Lady Queen of Heaven Parish Model

This model is interesting in several ways. It is the first model which comes from an experience that combines several parishes. It therefore makes the need for parish identification stronger in mystagogia activities. It is especially creative in its activities, and shows that learning happens in many ways other than discussion. It also exemplifies the deep commitment to prayerful re-

flection that is present throughout the RCIA experience for this team.

COMPOSITE MODEL: MYSTAGOGIA

Liturgical Celebrations
- Sunday Eucharist as a group.
- Sunday celebration with the bishop the week after Easter.
- Pentecost commitment ceremony, where neophytes publicly make their commitment to regular service in the Lord.

Parish Life
- Each neophyte is expected to make an on-going commitment to service in the parish family, both within the Church community and beyond it in some service ministry.
- Membership in an on-going small community is a high priority and the sponsor is to facilitate that commitment.

Broader Church Awareness
- Sunday celebration with the bishop on the second Sunday of Easter.
- Recognition of service beyond the parish boundaries as a necessary part of parish membership.

Spiritual Direction
- First experience of reconciliation.
- Encouragement to choose an on-going spiritual director.

**Composite Model:
Mystagogia Sessions**

Week #1: Reflection on the Events of Holy Week

Purpose
To share feelings about what happened during Holy Week, and what it feels like to be a full member.

Major Points
- What was your most memorable moment during the Triduum? (Include sponsors and team members in this discussion.)
- What were your feelings during the celebrations?
- How do you feel now?
- An extended time for prayer of praise is appropriate here.
- Explain purpose and plan for mystagogia: what it means to experience mystery; how to reflect on experiences together.

Note: Whenever possible, this should be held during Easter week.

Neophytes are usually anxious for this sharing, even though staff members deserve a vacation.

Week #2: Ministry of Evangelization

Purpose
To acknowledge the special charism for evangelization that new Catholics have; to describe some models for personal evangelization; to emphasize the importance of relational evangelization.

Major Points
- Getting in touch with how each person there was evangelized, and by whom.
- Naming evangelization—what makes something evangelization?
- Discussion of specific possibilities for evangelization; what it means to give witness.
- Challenge each person to invite someone to join the new catechumenate group.

References: *Invitation*, McBride, Chap. 21;
Converts, Dropouts, Returnees, Hoge;
On Evangelization in the Modern World, Pope Paul VI.

Week #3: Choosing a Ministry

Purpose
To help each neophyte see him/herself as a minister; to help each one make a commitment to some regular service to the local church.

Major Points
- We are ministers when we are acting out of Christian commitment, for the service of the Kingdom.
- Examples of ministry which is church-centered and ministry outside the Church.
- Helping each person make a commitment to some regular ministry.

Session Outline
1. What do you think of the word ministry? Whom do you know who is a minister?

2. Present ministry as our life response to our Christian commitment. Ministry has two dimensions—what we do formally in church, and what we do otherwise because of faith.

3. In groups of three to four, have sponsors and other experienced Catholics present tell of their ministry experience, and help each neophyte identify how he or she is experiencing a call to ministry.

4. With the total group, in a prayerful atmosphere, have each neophyte identify a decision for ministry, and call for prayer from the total community for them. It is good for this to be personal, calling each one to the center of the group, and laying hands on them as the prayer is said.

Reference: *Invitation*, McBride, Chap. 19, 20.
"Ministry", Scriptographics.

Week #4: Home Mass

Purpose
To experience Eucharist in an informal small group setting, and to have an opportunity to plan the celebration.

This may be in the home of a sponsor or team member; in the room where meetings were held; or in church, but around the altar or in a more intimate setting than parish Masses usually can be.

Planning for the celebration can include finding the readings of the day (show them how to do this) or choosing others with special meaning; choosing music that is appropriate and familiar; setting up the space; and planning the celebration to follow.

Be sure the Mass is informal, and not just a Sunday Eucharist with fewer people. Call for as much participation as possible, and allow it to happen.

Week #5: Always . . . Never . . . Most of the Time

Purpose
To suggest practical aspects of what it means to be a good Catholic.

Major Points
- Discuss perceptions of what Catholics should always do, what we should almost never do, and what we should do most of the time.
- Present basics of a Catholic lifestyle, with special attention to the Sacrament of Reconciliation, which will be available the next week.
- Present on-going resources for information—diocesan newspaper, libraries, texts, adult education programs.

Session Outline
1. List two people you consider very good Catholics; share your list, and discuss what makes them good Catholics.

2. In groups of four, discuss these three questions:
   What should Catholics almost always do?
   What should Catholics almost never do?
   What should Catholics do most of the time?

3. Share results of discussion with the total group.

4. Summarize and highlight—to be a good Catholic, one needs: on-going growth in prayer, study, and participation in community; responsibility for self (conscience), for the Church community, and for the world.

5. Describe parish and diocesan resources for continuing study and information.

Resources: Papal encyclicals
            Recent pastoral letters
            Documents of Vatican II
            Local Catholic newspaper
            Samples of Catholic magazines and national papers

Week #6: Reconciliation

Purpose
To provide an informal communal celebration of Reconciliation for an easy first experience of the sacrament.

Session Outline
1. Short review of why we have the Sacrament of Penance.

2. Celebrate communal Reconciliation:
   This suggested format assumes that two spaces are available for the service, one in church (or another place) where individual confession can be available; the other in a less formal room for the celebrating afterwards.

   Opening prayer
   Hymn
   Reading
   Psalm
   Gospel
   Homily
   Group examination of conscience
   Prayer of contrition
   Individual confession

   As each person leaves confession, he/she is greeted by a team member, and the personal sponsor; his/her hands are washed symbolically, near the baptismal

font; they then go to the other space, and wait in a relaxed and celebrating way, until everyone is ready to go on.
When all are finished, celebrants come to the celebration room, give a penance such as singing the Our Father together, and a closing blessing. The group then continues the celebration with refreshments and music.

Week #7 (final week): Closing Party

This may be a big party given by neophytes for all who have helped them over the whole process; or it may simply be their own time to say good-bye to one another. It should include some time for prayer, and a reminder that this is "the first day of the rest of your life."

OTHER MODELS
The Mystagogia Period
at Saint Augustine Parish (1982), Washington D.C.
Catechumenate Director: John Butler
Beginning the Sunday after Easter, we meet between the two morning Masses for mystagogia. The first week includes viewing slides of themselves at the Vigil and meditation on that event.

Over the next several meetings our purpose is to review the theology and symbolism of sacraments, to look back over the whole process and recall the major themes, and to focus on current ministry.

We talk together about termination, their separation from this small community and moving to the larger community, and what that means for them. They are invited to an on-going Scripture sharing once a month to continue the level of faith sharing they had achieved.

Shortly after Pentecost, there is a parish reunion of all the people received into the Church as adults.

In some years there is a second initiation celebrated on Pentecost for those people who were asked to wait before the election.

Mystagogia Period:
Our Lady Queen of Heaven Parish
New Orleans, Louisiana
Catechumenate Director: Pam Manual
Neophytes are featured in the issue of the parish newspaper immediately following Easter. Our purpose is to make sure that the whole parish is aware of our new members, and also to celebrate their initiation.

A highlight during mystagogia is the surprise gift to each neophyte of a photograph album with pictures of themselves and the others from their group throughout the previous year. Captions are included throughout the book, and each person then has a marvelous remembrance of the faith journey they have taken together.

We also use this activity based on the meaning of bread to help neophytes reflect on their journey together: Two bowls are placed on the table, one empty, and one containing a mixture of flour, salt and yeast in a proper proportion for making bread.

People are asked to reflect: Flour is the basic ingredient, that which makes it what it is. Who or what has been flour for you?

Salt is a formative ingredient, that which gives flavor to the bread. Who or what has been salt in your journey?

Yeast is the ingredient that changes all the others. Who or what has been yeast for you?

After reflecting on this for a short time, place some of the mixture into the empty bowl, and explain what you have done.

This mixture is then made into bread, and shared at the next session of the group.

These activities complement the three more formal sessions that are held with the group, in which they recall the meaning of the sacraments they have received, work through their personal call to ministry, and celebrate Eucharist together.

The final activity is a party, filled with joyful celebration.

(*Note:* Our Lady Queen of Heaven Parish involves people from five different parishes in their RCIA process, as catechumens, sponsors, and team members. They have discovered ways to share resources as well as initiate members into a parish community. Their average numbers are around 50.)

PARISH WORKSHEET
1. How will you design your mystagogia period?

2. How will you help neophytes choose an appropriate ministry?

3. How will you foster neophytes moving into on-going parish groups?

4. Who will have the energy and time to devote to leadership in this period?

5. How can you make the most of the evangelizing potential of the neophytes?

6. What kind of follow-up care will the new Catholic need?

7. How will you provide it?

Chapter VIII

The RCIA Experience: Celebrating the Rites

- ■ The Rites in the RCIA
- ■ Liturgy Planning for RCIA
- ■ Rites with the Already Baptized
- ■ Dismissal
- ■ Sample Rites

THE RITES IN THE RCIA

This chapter on the rites of the RCIA comes towards the end of this Manual. We have mentioned them, listed their names, and assumed that they were happening. Now we give proper attention to the rites as the central experiences of the RCIA process.

The RCIA is, after all, a liturgical document. To understand it properly, it must be seen as part of the liturgy of the Church.

This should challenge our practice of RCIA in several ways. Are the rites as central as they should be in your experience? Or are they just extras that you do along the way? Do your formation sessions and activities find meaning and expression in the rites? Or have the rites become another formation activity? Are the liturgy people in your parish (and your diocese) as involved in the RCIA as the catechetical leaders? Or has the RCIA been taken over by one or the other?

In this chapter, the rites take center stage. Each parish RCIA team must understand them well, and find in them the purpose and meaning for the way they plan to do RCIA. It is this proper understanding of the rites that keeps us on track in RCIA.

The rites are supposed to celebrate what is happening for people. If it is not happening, it cannot be celebrated. Each period should reflect the liturgical stage of the participant. So, what happens in precatechumenate prepares for the rite of acceptance into the order of catechumens. What happens in catechumenate assumes the rite of acceptance into the order of catechumens and prepares for the rite of election, and so on. Keeping those rites as the focus in our planning will help insure that we are progressing appropriately through the RCIA.

Highlighting the Rites in the Total Process

Evangelization

Precatechumenate
RECEIVING INTERESTED INQUIRERS (#39)
SUITABLE PRAYERS (#40)
*RITE OF ACCEPTANCE INTO THE ORDER OF CATE-CHUMENS (#48–74; 505–529)

Catechumenate
BLESSINGS (#95–97)
EXORCISMS (#90–94)
ANOINTING (#98–103)
GIVING A CHRISTIAN NAME (#73; 200–202)
*RITE OF ELECTION (#106–137; 530–561)

Enlightenment/Purification
SCRUTINIES (#141–146; 150–156; 164–177)
PRESENTATIONS (#147–149; 157–162; 178–183)
PREPARATORY RITES (#185–205)
*INITIATION (#206–243; 566–594)

Mystagogia
CLOSING CEREMONY (237)

(* = Major Rites)

RECEIVING INTERESTED INQUIRERS is to be a simple celebration such as introducing people who have shown some interest in the Church. They could be asked to stand at the end of Mass, and be greeted with applause, or they could be called to the front, and blessed or prayed over. National Statutes, #1 emphasizes that this is to be entirely informal.

SUITABLE PRAYERS during precatechumenate should also be characterized by simplicity. They are appropriate when it would be helpful to recognize the connection inquirers already have with the Church. Such prayers would ordinarily happen if the period were especially long, or if there were special problems for particular inquirers.

THE RITE OF ACCEPTANCE INTO THE ORDER OF CATE-CHUMENS ritualizes the person's acceptance of Jesus, and the decision to become a catechumen. It is also the time when the Church makes a very special commitment to these people.

Note that this rite happens before the liturgy of the word. As soon as the community is gathered (just after the opening prayer), the inquirers are presented to the community. Inquirers can be waiting outside, and the community or representatives of the community can go out to greet them with the opening dialogue; or they can be in the back of church, with the community invited to turn around to welcome them; they might symbolically knock on the door of the church to request entrance. How it is done, their position in the church and the calling of their name should symbolize that they are outside and requesting to come in. The community should likewise express symbolically their welcome to them.

The dialogue with the celebrant should be a natural and real conversation. Each person should have the opportunity to answer individually, offering his/her reasons for wanting to be part of the Church. And each person should be signed with the sign of the cross.

It is appropriate to give some gift to catechumens at this point. The National Statutes suggest that a cross be presented.

BLESSINGS and minor EXORCISMS can be done formally or informally, in the Sunday liturgical setting, or in connection with some other activity of the group. They are short and simple prayers on behalf of the catechumen, and can be done by ordained or lay people. If they are done on a Sunday, they could be experienced as a more elaborate than usual blessing at the point of dismissal. At the conclusion of a formation session or other meeting of the group, the blessing may be in the form of a more ritualized closing prayer time. The exorcisms should be connected to discussions or problems with evil, and the blessings to discussions or experiences of our need for God's goodness.

ANOINTING WITH THE OIL OF CATECHUMENS can be done alone or in connection with another rite. It can be done several times or only once as part of preparatory rites on Holy Saturday. It brings with it the wisdom and strength needed on the journey to Baptism.

GIVING A CHRISTIAN NAME is a rite that can be done at any one of a variety of times, or may be eliminated entirely. It should express the reality of the new life beginning for the catechumen, as well as some sense of direction in the new life. Those choosing the name of a saint as their Christian name should do so because of some desired virtue or lifestyle exhibited by the saint. They should be able to explain why a particular saint was chosen. Sponsors are often able to suggest appropriate patrons for a catechumen or candidate.

It is not necessary for a person to choose a new name. Those who would prefer not to may also recognize a new life beginning by understanding a new significance to their old name. (As in: "Jane, your name takes on new significance today as God uses it to call you to his Church.")

THE RITE OF ELECTION is the turning point of the whole catechumenate process. It is the time when God calls (elects) the catechumen to membership in the Church. Thus the election is God's call which is heard in the call of the Church. On the part of the catechumen, the rite of election expresses a final decision to enter the Church. Each of these two actions should be symbolized clearly in the celebration.

The first action is the election by the Church. It involves "testimony" or affirmation given by members of the community on behalf of the catechumens. This is in reality the culmination of the discernment that has been going on in preparation for this rite. People from the community should be willing to identify the changes that have occurred in the catechumen, and the community should have the chance to signify its acceptance of each new member.

The decision of the catechumens is signified by their signing their name in the book of the elect, and that action and that book should be clearly significant. Usually, the rite of election happens at the Cathedral Church, with the bishop as minister. There is a preliminary *sending rite* that is suggested for the parish to use in the morning as its part in this celebration.

SCRUTINIES show our need to continually measure our lives in light of the gospel. They are about the battle against evil in the life of the Church. The spirit of the scrutiny should be solemn and prayerful. The call for prayer in silence is significant, and a posture of prayer is most appropriate—kneeling, bowing the head, extending hands. The image of the elect in the midst of the community should also be clear. The exorcisms that are part of the scrutinies are done by an ordained minister, and his action should also be clear and central.

PRESENTATIONS entrust our most precious gifts to these new members. The creed is symbol of our faith, and when we share it with these people we should be sharing all that our faith means to us. Consider having the parish council or other leaders in the parish do this rite, to help them recognize their personal ownership of the Church, and also the need for them to know and accept these new members. The Lord's Prayer is a gift we all need to appreciate more and more throughout our lives. The rite should have meaning for all who participate in it, baptized and unbaptized alike, long-time member, returning member, or soon to be member.

PREPARATORY RITES should be focused on the coming celebration of initiation rather than major events themselves. They include a reading from God's Word, homily, recitation of the creed, and *ephphata*.

INITIATION should happen at the Easter Vigil, and involves Baptism, Confirmation, and Eucharist for catechumens, and the Reception into Full Communion, Confirmation and Eucharist for the already baptized. Because the Easter Vigil is such an involved celebration, it is essential that the initiation rites are clear in the planning for this night. Remember that most missalettes and other planning aids for the Vigil do not present sufficient material for the initiation section. The parish team must coordinate the unbaptized adult, the unbaptized children, the baptized adults, and the renewal of Baptism promises for the community, each of which has different aspects.

A CLOSING CEREMONY on or near Pentecost should formally end the RCIA process. There is no specific suggestion for the form of this. Many parishes connect it with the commitment to ministry that is appropriate for the neophyte at this time.

LITURGY PLANNING FOR RCIA

Celebrating the rites is the way we mark the stages of the conversion journey. It provides the context in which the community and the individual ritualize what is happening.

The formulas for the rites as written are meant to give the framework for a local parish celebration. The introduction provides the understanding of what is to be symbolized in the rite. The team must study both, to prepare for the specific local celebration.

Remember that the rites are:

1. Significant experiences in the conversion journey;

2. The best opportunity to involve the largest number of parishioners;

3. A call to the team to recognize individuals and the reality of their journey.

Planning the Rites in Your Parish

Study the introduction and basic flow of the rite to understand what is being celebrated in it.

Consider the catechumens in your parish, and what is happening in their lives.

Consider your parish, and how it acts as a community.

Using the basic outline of the rite, plan the celebration to express the conversion experience of your catechumens, and the community life of your parish.

Allow for personal statements of faith wherever possible rather than repeated short answers. In the rite of acceptance into the order of catechumens the question, "What do you ask of the Church?" is posed. Allow catechumens to create their own response if they choose, rather than simply answering "Baptism" or "Faith."

Call for parish and parishioner participation wherever possible. For example, have sponsors sign the catechumens at the rite of acceptance into the order of catechumens, invite the whole community to pray with extended hands in the scrutinies.

Involve other ministers in the participation in the rite—music ministers, ushers, lectors, etc.

Be aware of movement, placement, visibility and audibility for the congregation. You may have to use microphones. Usually, plan to have the catechumens and sponsors face the congregation, rather than standing in front with their backs to the people.

Be well prepared, but not well rehearsed. Something is happening during the rite; it is not a performance.

Plan each year. Special care is needed to assure that the rites are new and personal for each new group, and not simply a matter of "doing the rites" or even "doing what worked well last year".

Consider the whole celebration, not just the one aspect you are planning. For instance, if there is a prayer for catechumens as part of the rite, it can replace the prayer of the faithful that day. The choice and placement of music should reflect what is happening. Having the activity well choreographed will keep the action flowing, and the time commitment reasonable. In this way, most of the rites can be done without adding any extra time to Mass. The first two major rites (rite of becoming a catechumen and the rite of election) do add extra time. People should be prepared for that, and the action should be particularly well planned so that it flows smoothly.

Planning for Diocesan Celebrations

While the parish celebrations of the rites are primary, most parishes and dioceses also find it helpful to celebrate some of the rites with others. The most significant time when this should happen is at the rite of election, of which the bishop is the ordinary minister. (The parish celebrates a rite of sending the catechumens for election).

Dioceses have also joined together for other rites such as: A blessing by the bishop early in the catechumenate period; the presentation of the creed on the second Sunday of Lent; preparatory rites on Holy Saturday morning; Mass of Thanksgiving with the bishop sometime during mystagogia. (Any one of a variety of days could be appropriate: the Sunday after Easter, Ascension Thursday, the Vigil of Pentecost, or Pentecost Day itself.)

The benefits of these larger gatherings include: the

experience of the larger Church; the chance to share with other catechumens; the involvement of the bishop, and the exercise of his role as primary teacher; and the good feeling of seeing how many people are joining this community.

For more information about planning to celebrate the rites, see:

DiGidio, *RCIA The Rites Revisited.*

*Dujarier, *The Rites of Christian Initiation.*
This book is particularly helpful in coming to understand the meaning behind the rites, and giving suggestions for interpreting the rites to local circumstances.

Hackett, "Adult Initiation: Selected Music for the Celebrations of the Rites", *C.I.R.* II, Connections G.

Parker, "The Environment for Initiation", *C.I.R.* II, Enlightenment B.

RCIA, Appendix II.

Sokol, "Liturgy as a Conversion Moment", *C.I.R.* IV, Connections F.

RITES WITH THE ALREADY BAPTIZED

When the RCIA was first published in Latin in 1972, it included the Rite of Reception of Baptized Christians into Full Communion With the Catholic Church, and chapter 4 of the RCIA was called "Baptized, Uncatechized Catholics." In the U.S., most people coming to the Catholic Church requesting membership fit that first category, and so that part was translated into English before the rest of the RCIA. In 1974, when the RCIA became available in English, it did not include the Rite of Reception into Full Communion, and never referred to it. Unfortunately, many people who used the RCIA did not know about the Rite of Reception into Full Communion, and as a result often treated those baptized Christians in exactly the same way they treated catechumens.

Today's English translation clearly shows the relationships and distinctions between and among catechumens (those unbaptized adults coming to membership) [Part I, #1–251], candidates for reception into full communion with the Catholic Church (those baptized Christians coming to membership) [Part II, Chap. 5, #473–504], and uncatechized adults preparing for confirmation and eucharist (those baptized Catholics preparing to complete their sacramental initiation) [Part II, Chap. 4, #400–472]. A most helpful addition in the document produced for the church in the U.S. is the material in Appendix I which gives sample rites that combine the various groups.

There are many similarities among the three groups, and often there is benefit to invite them to share many of the experiences of the RCIA together. They are all on a conversion journey. They are all preparing for full membership in the Catholic community of faith. They are all responding to a call to deeper awareness and relationship with Jesus. They all can share their conversion experience with the community through celebrating public rites. They all need one another for encouragement and strength on the journey.

The differences among them are significant, however, and while much can be shared, it is important to make the distinctions that respect the baptism of those who have already begun their life in the Lord.

The descriptive titles from the new translation are: catechumens, candidates for confirmation and eucharist, and candidates for reception into full communion.

In planning and thinking, teams should get used to dealing with "catechumens and candidates", not simply catechumens. Many parishes use the terms "catechumen" and "catechumenate" to include more than their technical meaning. Thus "catechumenate concerns" often refer to concerns of the total RCIA, and not just the catechumenate period; and the term "catechumen" is used for participants throughout the RCIA process, both already baptized and unbaptized.

When this is done, it is very important that the distinctions still be understood, and that planning still is distinctive for the two groups.

For more information on the question of including the already baptized in rites of the RCIA, see:

Forum (newsletter, North American Forum on the Catechumenate), Vol. II, #2 and 3

RCIA, Appendix I.

DISMISSAL

Dismissal refers to the practice of sending catechumens to a further experience of the Word of God within community, rather than having them remain for the Liturgy of the Eucharist. It should begin with the rite of acceptance into the order of catechumens and continue through to full initiation. This practice in the early history of the Church is why the Mass used to be divided into "Mass of the Catechumens," and "Mass of the Faithful."

This practice has meaning for us today because:

1. The liturgy of the Word and catechumens belong together. It is the center of their formation within the community, and their formal participation in it remains a sign to the rest of the community.

2. While catechumens can actively participate in this further experience of the Word, they cannot participate in the Liturgy of the Eucharist.

3. There is a dramatic effect on the community that remains, clearly showing the value of full membership, and the position of the Eucharist in our community.

4. It is an expression of our faith in God's presence in his Word.

As you prepare for dismissal in your parish, consider these factors:

Parish leaders have the greatest effect on the attitude of the parish and the catechumens toward this practice. It is usually hard to begin, because the idea of dismissing people sounds unhospitable, and we are so used to being hospitable. However, catechumens who have experienced it recognize that it is much better than staying for Eucharist, and not being able to receive. In addition, catechumens expect us to tell them what is involved in becoming a member; if dismissal is part of it and is presented in a positive way, they accept it.

The success of dismissal depends largely on what catechumens are dismissed to. Certainly, it should not be to coffee and donuts and waiting for the end of the Mass. The purpose is further feeding on the Word of God, as it was broken open in the Liturgy of the Word.

Dismissal should be the normal practice; however, exceptions can be made for pastoral reasons. They should not be easy or frequent however, because of what the person would miss along the conversion journey. Remember, even those who who have been regularly attending Mass before becoming a catechumen have been doing so as guests; dismissal is actually the first step to really belonging.

The idea must be explained to the parish community before it begins, and the effect on the community should be regularly addressed.

For further reading on the question of dismissal, see:

Simcoe, Mary Ann, "All Catechumens Depart", *Chicago Catechumenate*, Vol. 4, No. 3.

Dismissal: How To Do It
RCIA #67 gives this and other wordings:
"Catechumens, go in peace and may the Lord remain with you always."
Response: "Thanks be to God."
Some questions to consider as you plan how to do the rite of dismissal:

1. *Where will those to be dismissed be seated?*

When they are seated in a group, they can easily be asked to stand together, and then leave in a group for their study. If they have been scattered throughout the church, it may be preferable to call them to stand before the community and then dismiss them.

2. *At what point in the liturgy will they be dismissed?*

The RCIA calls for dismissal after the homily, and before the recitation of the Creed. Some parishes prefer to have this movement while other movement is going on, for instance while the collection is being taken. Their choice then is to dismiss after the prayer of the faithful. The former is more in conformity with the ancient practice, but the spirit of the rite can be sustained with a later dismissal.

It is a good sign to have the catechumens place their offerings in a basket on their way out of the church. It is an expression of their real membership in the Church, both for them and the community.

3. *Who will go with the catechumens?*

Many parishes choose to dismiss only catechumens, candidates, and a discussion leader. Other possibilities include sponsors, family members, and team members, as well as the discussion leader. Those fully initiated Catholics who may be dismissed as sponsors or team members must appreciate the real presence of Jesus in his Word as well as the Sacrament of Eucharist, since they will also be fasting from Eucharist, unless they choose to participate in another celebration.

Some parishes give a simple blessing to the leader for the session, similar to the blessing given to the deacon before he proclaims the gospel.

4. *What is the relationship between the faith sharing after dismissal and other catechetical sessions for the catechumenate?*

Some parishes identify the two, others separate them in time. They should always be connected in experience. The faith sharing that occurs during the time after dismissal is a specially graced time, and it has the Word of God as its special power. Usually, it is in that context that catechumens find themselves challenged to change and grow, when they can identify the nature of their conversion experience. The power that directs that time can flow over to catechetical sessions, even though they may happen on another day of the week. Connecting whatever is discussed with the Sunday experience, and, where possible, with the sharing that followed it, gives a desired focus to whatever else is happening during the week for catechumens.

5. *How long should the sessions last?*

Many parishes schedule their formation sessions at this time. They begin with reflection on the Word, and use that as the basis for catechetical input. They would have to schedule a substantial period of time at this point, and then usually do not schedule a separate session during the week.

Other parishes spend this time just in further reflection on the Word, and schedule other sessions during the week. They are then able to call the catechumens back to the community after Communion. In that way, they hear the general parish announcements, and can take part in the fellowship after the liturgy. A benefit of this is that family members are able to go home together. A problem is that the time for sharing among catechumens and candidates is very limited.

6. *Should candidates be dismissed along with catechumens?*

Because candidates for full communion are not able to participate fully in the Liturgy of the Eucharist by receiving Communion, it is most appropriate to dismiss them along with the catechumens. The spirit of worship and prayer that flows into the sharing after dismissal has its effect on all who participate in it.

SAMPLE RITES

Presentation of the Creed (#157–163)
(In this model the presentation is made by the Parish Council. It may be in the context of a Sunday Eucharist, or a Parish Council meeting, or a welcome dinner for the catechumens. The leader should be the chairperson of the Council.)

Leader: *Let the elect now come forward to receive the creed from the Church.*

These words embody the faith we hold. As we entrust them to you, so we count you as true brothers and sisters in faith. Listen carefully to the words by which you are to be justified. The words are few, but the mysteries they contain are awe inspiring. Accept them with a sincere heart and be faithful to them.

Members of the Council hand over copies of the Creed and stand encircling the elect. They lead all present in reciting the Nicene Creed.

Leader: *Let us pray for our brothers and sisters who have been chosen for membership in our Church, that God in his mercy may make them responsive to his love, forgive their sins, and give them life in Christ Jesus our Lord.*

All pray in silence for a short time.

Council members then extend hands over the elect, saying together: *Father, all-powerful and ever-living God, fountain of light and truth, source of eternal love, hear our prayers for these elect. Cleanse them of sin, make them holy, give them true knowledge, firm hope and sound teaching so that they will be prepared for the grace of membership in the Church. We ask this through Christ our Lord. Amen.*

The copy of the Creed given to the elect should be attractive, so that it shows the value to be attributed to it. Hand lettering or special quality paper could be used. Attractive copies are also available for purchase from several religious articles stores.

Either the Nicene Creed or the Apostles' Creed may be presented. This model chooses the Nicene Creed because of its liturgical use.

Scrutinies (#150–156; 164–177)
The scrutinies are scheduled for the third, fourth, and fifth Sundays of Lent, with Cycle A readings. The prayers of each week reflect the gospel of that day. Parishes with elect are expected to use Cycle A readings each year.

If a parish does not use Cycle A readings in a given year, it is still possible to adjust a scrutiny so that it can be celebrated meaningfully. For instance, the second scrutiny is scheduled for the fourth Sunday of Lent, with the gospel story of the man born blind. It can be adjusted to be a first scrutiny on the second Sunday of Lent in Cycle B or C, with the gospel story of the transfiguration in this way:
After the homily, invite the elect to come forward. They and the congregation kneel and pray silently for a short time. Congregation stands for prayer of the faithful, while the elect remain kneeling.
Continue with prayers of #167, but adjust the closing prayer in this way:

Let us pray. Father of mercy, you showed yourself in true glory in the transfiguration of your Son, to help us to believe in him, and through that faith to reach the light of your kingdom. Free your chosen ones from any falsehood that surrounds them and keeps them from seeing your true light. Let truth be the foundation of their lives. May they live in your light forever. We ask this through Christ our Lord. Amen.

Celebrant lays hands on each in silence; then, with hands extended: *Lord Jesus, you are the true light that enlightens all men and women. By the Spirit of truth, free all who struggle against evil and untruth. Arouse the good will of these men and women whom you have chosen for your sacraments. Grant them to enjoy your light like those who witnessed your transfiguration, and inspire them to become fearless witnesses to the faith, for you are Lord forever and ever. Amen.*

Go in peace until we meet again. May the Lord be with you always.

Preparatory Rites—

(Used with several parishes coming together with the bishop on Holy Saturday morning.)

Welcome
Explanation and Introductions
Opening Hymn: *Amazing Grace*
Ephphata (#197–199); first half, opening the ears
Reading: Mark 7:31–37
Teaching from the Bishop
Ephphata; second half, opening the mouth

Sharing of faith among the elect—discussion in groups of about seven each, "What are your feelings now as your Baptism and entrance into the Church is so close?" (about 30 minutes.)

Recitation of the Creed (#195–196)

Reading from St. Cyril of Jerusalem on the significance of the Creed:
Within these verses are contained all instruction in the faith. This is what I want you to retain verbatim, and which each of you must carefully recite, without writing it on paper, but by engraving it by memory in your hearts. Keep this faith as the only provision you need for your journey all the rest of your life, and receive no other. See now, my brothers and sisters, and keep the

traditions which you now receive and write them in bold letters within your hearts.

Invitation to all catechumens to stand and recite the Nicene Creed from memory.

Hymn: *Lord's Prayer*

Exorcism (#94: A, E, H or K)
Call the elect forward for the exorcism; remind them of its significance as protection from evil.

Closing Blessing (#204)

Sign of Peace

Sample Rites: also see—

Hart, "The Rite of Becoming a Catechumen", *C.I.R.*, Vol I, Pre-Catechumenate D.

Hart, "The Rite of Election" *C.I.R.* I, Enlightenment A.

Hart, "The Rites of the Scrutinies and the Presentations", *C.I.R.* I, Enlightenment E.

Huck and Simcoe, *A Triduum Sourcebook.*

Huck, *The Three Days.*

Lewinski, Ron, "Homily for Ascension Day Mass of Thanksgiving", *Chicago Catechumenate* Vol. 4, No. 4.

Mitchell, "Exorcism in the RCIA", *C.I.R.*, I, Enlightenment D.

Naughton, "Election and Mystagogical Mass: Two Archdiocesan Celebrations", *C.I.R.* IV, Enlightenment A.

Vigna, "Rhythm of Eucharist, Rhythm of Lent", *C.I.R.*, II, Enlightenment I.

PARISH WORKSHEET

1. How will the RCIA Team relate to the Liturgy planners in your parish?
2. Who on your team will do special study of the rites, and make suggestions for local implementation?
3. How will the priest celebrant get to know the catechumens and candidates personally?
4. What rites will be celebrated by other ministers (deacons, catechists, etc.)?
5. How will participants be prepared for the rites?
   Catechumens and candidates?
   sponsors?
   celebrant?
   assembly?
6. How will you clarify the distinction between catechumens and the already baptized?
7. When are you able to participate with other parishes? How will the bishop be part of the initiation of catechumens from your community?
8. How will you evaluate the celebration of the rites?
9. How will you insure the unity of the catechetical experience you are providing with the liturgical celebrations?

Chapter IX

Resources

- Bibliography
- Places
- People
- Arts
- Audio-Visual Aids
- Special Groups

BIBLIOGRAPHY
RITE OF CHRISTIAN INITIATION OF ADULTS
Barbernitz, Patricia, *RCIA: What It Is; How It Works*, Liguori Publications, One Liguori Drive, Liguori, MO 63057, 1984. Practical look at the RCIA and what it means for the parish community.

Boyack, Kenneth, CSP, *A Parish Guide to Adult Initiation*, Paulist Press, 997 Macarthur Blvd., Mahwah, NJ, 07430, 1980. This book describes team roles in detail, and suggests how a parish could prepare for the first year's experience of RCIA.

DiGidio, Sandra, OSM, *RCIA The Rites Revisited*, Winston Press, 430 Oak Grove, Minneapolis, MN 55403, 1984. Presents ideas for adapting the rites from modern experiences.

Duggan, Robert, *Conversion and the Catechumenate*, Paulist Press, 997 Macarthur Blvd. Mahwah, NJ, 07430, 1984. A series of articles looking at the experience of conversion, as it is understood in the RCIA.

Dujarier, Rev. Michel, *A History of the Catechumenate*, William H. Sadlier, Inc., 11 Park Place, New York, NY 10007, 1979. Presents the story of the first centuries of the catechumenate.

Dujarier, Rev. Michel, *The Rites of Christian Initiation*, William H. Sadlier, Inc., 11 Park Place, New York, NY, 10007, 1979. Presents the significance of each of the rites of the RCIA, and gives suggestions for planning for local celebrations.

Dunning, James B., *New Wine, New Wineskins*, William H. Sadlier Inc., 11 Park Place, New York, NY, 10007, 1981. Presents the spirit and application of RCIA for local implementation. Emphasizes the ministries needed for successful implementation.

Fowler, James W., *Stages of Faith*, Harper and Row Publishers, Inc., 1700 Montgomery St., San Francisco, CA 94111, 1981. Classic presentation of the process of conversion for adults. Part IV is especially relevant for RCIA ministry.

Groome, Thomas H., *Christian Religious Education*, Harper and Row Publishers, Inc., 1700 Montgomery St., San Francisco, CA 94111, 1980. Presents a model for adult religious education based on sharing story and vision; most appropriate in the RCIA.

Kemp, Raymond B., *A Journey in Faith*, William H. Sadlier, 11 Park Place, New York, NY 10007, 1979. This book presents the early stages of RCIA implementation at St. Augustine Parish in Washington, D.C. A good resource for a beginning team.

Lewinski, Ron, *Guide for Sponsors*, Liturgy Training Publications, Archdiocese of Chicago, 1800 North Hermitage Ave., Chicago, IL 60622, 1980. This book is appropriate to give to potential sponsors to help them grasp the spirit of the ministry they are asked to accept.

Lewinski, Ron, *Welcoming the New Catholic*, Liturgy Training Publications, Archdiocese of Chicago, 1800 North Hermitage Ave., Chicago, IL 60622, 1978. Introduces the reader to the RCIA with a short 47 page booklet.

Made, Not Born, New Perspectives on Christian Initiation and the Catechumenate, The Murphy Center for Liturgical Research, University of Notre Dame

Press, Notre Dame IN 46556, 1976. A series of articles describing the beginning implementation of the RCIA in modern times. Chapters 1, 6, 7, 8 are especially helpful for the person beginning to implement the RCIA.

Powell, Karen Hinman and Joseph Sinwell, *Breaking Open the Word of God*, Cycle A; Cycle B; Cycle C, Paulist Press, 997 Macarthur Blvd., Mahwah, NJ, 17430. Resources for using the lectionary for catechesis in the RCIA.

Reedy, William J., ed., *Becoming a Catholic Christian*, William H. Sadlier Inc., 11 Park Place, New York, NY, 10007, 1978. A series of articles out of the Senaque Symposium on the RCIA, which was effectively the beginning of modern RCIA ministry.

Rite of Christian Initiation of Adults, 1988. Official document for the RCIA in the United States. The Rite is available through several publishers in ritual and study editions. It is in an easy to read format through Liturgy Training Publications, 1800 Hermitage Ave., Chicago, IL 60622–1101.

Searl, Mark, *Christening, The Making of Christians*, The Liturgical Press, Collegeville, MN 56321, 1980. Applies the principles of initiation and Church membership to our sacramental practice. Emphasizes the progressive initiation of children.

Wilde, James, *A Catechumenate Needs Everybody: Study Guides for Parish Ministers*, Liturgy Training Publications, 1800 North Hermitage Ave., Chicago, IL 60622–1101, 1988. Each of 20 chapters describes a task related to Christian initiation; the pages are perforated for easy duplication.

Wilde, James, *Finding and Forming Sponsors and Godparents*, Liturgy Training Publications, 1800 Hermitage Ave., Chicago, IL 60622–1101, 1988. Includes a brief history of the roles of sponsors and godparents, and recruiting methods and the qualifications from moral and canonical perspectives.

Periodicals

Christian Initiation Resources, William H. Sadlier, Inc., 11 Park Place, New York, NY, 10007, Volumes I, II, III, IV, 1980–1984. Published quarterly; articles designed to help implement the RCIA, and restore it to a central position in parish life. Each volume is divided into five sections, Precatechumenate, Catechumenate, Enlightenment, Mystagogia, and Connections. (Many of the articles from these volumes have been reprinted, and are now available as *Christian Initiation Resources Reader*, same publisher.)

Catechumenate, Liturgy Training Publications, Archdiocese of Chicago, 1800 North Hermitage Ave., Chicago, IL 60622. Published five times a year;

includes articles and reviews which foster the implementation of the RCIA.

Forum, North American Forum on the Catechumenate newsletter, 3017 4th Street NE, Washington D.C., 20017. Articles, reviews, and resources of interest to RCIA ministers.

Evangelization Bibliography

Bohr, Rev. David, *Evangelization in America: Proclamation, Way of Life, and the Catholic Church in America*, Paulist Press, 997 Macarthur Blvd., Mahwah, NJ 07430, 1977. Explores the evangelization mission of the American Church today.

Boyack, Kenneth, CSP, *Catholic Evangelization Today*, Paulist Press, 997 Macarthur Blvd., Mahwah, NJ, 17430. A contemporary meditation and reflection on Catholic evangelization today.

Hale, Dr. J. Russell, *Who Are the Unchurched?*, Glenmary Research Center, 4606 East-West Highway, Washington, D.C., 20014, 1978. Analyzes conversations with 165 unchurched persons.

Hoge, Dean R. *Converts, Dropouts, Returnees: A Study of Religious Change Among Catholics*, The Pilgrim Press, 132 W. 31 Street, New York, NY 10001, 1981. Results of interviews with 200 people who had recently entered or left the Catholic Church.

McKee, Rev. William, C.SS.R., *How to Reach Out to Inactive Catholics*, Liguori Publications, One Liguori Drive, Liguori, MO 63057. Practical parish program based on work with 4,000 inactive Catholics.

Paul VI, Pope, *On Evangelization in the Modern World (Evangelii Nuntiandi)*, USCC Publications Office, 1312 Massachusetts Avenue N.W., Washington, D.C., 20005, 1976. Basic statement and description of the evangelization mission of the Catholic Church.

Rauff, Edward A., *Why People Join the Church*, The Pilgrim Press, 132 West 31 Street, New York, NY 10001, 1979. Study focusing on the spiritual journeys of 180 men and women which led them to the Church.

Roozen, Dr. David, *The Churched and Unchurched American*, Glenmary Research Center, 4606 East-West Highway, Washington, D.C. 20014, 1978. Comparative profile based on interviews with Catholics, Protestants and the unchurched.

Smith, Dr. Glen, *Evangelizing Adults; Evangelizing Youth*, Paulist National Catholic Evangelization Association, 3031 4th Street, NE, Washington, D.C. 20017, 1985. Presents models from Protestant and Catholic groups active in evangelization.

Periodicals

Catholic Evangelization in The United States of America, published bimonthly by Paulist National Catholic

Evangelization Association, 3031 Fourth Street, N.E., Washington, D.C., 20017.

Other Materials

The Paulist National Catholic Evangelization Association (3031 Fourth Street, N.E., Washington, D.C. 20017) also has many articles, materials, and case studies available for use by individuals and parishes.

Adult Catechisms

Anderson, William A., *In His Light*, William C. Brown Company Publishers, 2460 Kerper Blvd., Dubuque, IA 52001, 1979. (208 pages). A companion volume, *Journeying In His Light*, provides deeper insight by providing additional Scripture for reflection, suggestions to encourage personal reflection, and structures for faith sharing experiences.

Chilson, Richard, C.S.P., *Catholic Christianity*, Paulist Press, 997 Macarthur Blvd., Mahwah, NJ 07430, 1987. A comprehensive guidebook to Catholic Christianity designed for those entering the church or for anyone seeking a new awareness of the church.

Foley, Leonard, O.F.M., *Believing in Jesus: A Popular Overview of the Catholic Faith*, St. Anthony Messenger Press, 1615 Republic Street, Cincinnati, OH 45210, 1983. (185 pages). Uses a heavily biblical approach. Now selling at the rate of 5,000 copies per month.

Gallagher, Rev. Joseph V., C.S.P., *To Be a Catholic: A Catechism for Today (Para Ser Catolico - Un Catecismo Para Hoy)*, Paulist Press, 997 Macarthur Blvd., Mahwah, NJ 07430. Post Vatican II theology in simple question and answer format. Available in English and in Spanish.

Guzie, Tad, *What the Eucharist Means to Catholic Families;* and *What Confirmation Means to Catholic Families*, Claretian Publications, 221 West Madison Street, Chicago, IL 60606, 1983. (24 pages each). These pamphlets are widely used in parishes to help involve parents in sacrament preparation. They are inexpensive, and an ideal tool to reach large numbers of families in a clear, accessible style.

Hellwig, Monika, *Understanding Catholicism*, Paulist Press, 997 Macarthur Blvd., Mahwah, NJ 07430. Examines all the great Catholic doctrines, showing the historical conditions they arose from, and the meaning they have in the religious search of thoughtful people today.

Kenny, John, C.S.P., *Now That You Are a Catholic*, Paulist Press, 997 Macarthur Blvd., Mahwah, NJ 07430, 1977. Practices, traditions, customs of Catholics for the newcomer.

Kohmescher, Matthew F., *Catholicism Today: A Survey of Catholic Belief and Practice*, Paulist Press, 997

Macarthur Blvd., Mahwah, NJ 07430. Easy-to-read basic introduction to Catholic teaching on theological and social matters of general concern. For classroom and individual use. Includes bibliography and discussion questions.

Lawler, Ronald, O.F.M. Cap. and others, ed., *The Teaching of Christ*, Our Sunday Visitor, Inc., Noll Plaza, Huntington, IN 46750, 1976. A Catholic catechism for adults, including extensive indexes and supplements.

Malloy, Rev. Joseph, C.S.P., *Catechism for Inquirers*, Paulist Press, 997 Macarthur Blvd., Mahwah NJ 07430, 1976. Introduction and explanation of the teachings of the Catholic Church.

McBride, Rev. Alfred, *Invitation*, Paulist National Catholic Evangelization Association, 3031 Fourth Street, N.E., Washington, D.C. 20017, 1984. (26 chapters, 4 pages each) Basic introduction to the faith of Catholics, in a format easily usable for RCIA, returning Catholics, or parish adult education programs.

Redemptorist Pastoral Publication, *Handbook for Today's Catholic (Manual Para El Catolico De Hoy)*, Liguori Publications, One Liguori Drive, Liguori, MO 63057, 1983. (64 pages) The book is arranged in three sections: beliefs, practices, prayers. Available in English and in Spanish.

Redemptorist Pastoral Publications, *Handbook for Today's Catholic Family (Manual Para La Familia Catolica Hispana De Hoy)*, Liguori Publications, One Liguori Drive, Liguori MO 63057, 1980. (96 pages) Arranged in three sections: basic foundations, basic prayers, basic resources. Available in English and in Spanish.

Redemptorist Pastoral Publications, *The Illustrated Catechism*, Liguori Publications, One Liguori Drive, Liguori, MO 63057, 1983. (112 pages) Divided into five sections: The Christian Vision, The Church, The Sacraments, The Dignity of the Christian, Prayer; and a supplement on the Church in history, at prayer, and the law of the Church.

Redemptorist Pastoral Publications, *Your Faith (Tu Fe)*, Liguori Publications, One Liguori Drive, Liguori, MO 63057, 1983. (64 pages) Divided into seventeen short sections. Available in English and in Spanish.

Scriptographics Booklets, various titles, Channing L. Bete Co., Inc., 200 State Road, South Deerfield, MA 01373. Booklets available on most areas of the Catholic faith, characterized by simplicity, readability, and illustrations.

White, Thomas, and Desmond O'Donnell, OMI, *Renewal of Faith*, Ave Maria Press, Notre Dame, IN 46556, 1974. (240 pages) Prayer and Scripture based adult catechism designed for individual and group use. Purpose is to renew faith in Jesus Christ and commitment to the Church as the Christian community. Nine chapters, each followed by points for discussion and questions for review.

Wintz, Fr. Jack, O.F.M., Ed. *Catholic Update*, St. Anthony Messenger Press, 1615 Republic Street, Cincinnati, OH 45210. Published monthly on questions of interest to adult Catholics.

Related Material

Church Documents

Called and Gifted, The American Catholic Laity, USCC Publications, 1312 Massachusetts Ave., Washington, D.C. 20005.

Code of Canon Law, Latin-English Edition, Canon Law Society of America, Washington, D.C. 20064, 1983.

Documents of Vatican II, "Constitution On the Sacred Liturgy", "Dogmatic Constitution on the Church", "Decree on the Apostolate of the Laity", America Press, 1966.

Renewing the Earth, Catholic Documents on Peace, Justice, and Liberation, Image Books, Doubleday & Co., Inc., Garden City, NY, 1977.

Sharing the Light of Faith, National Catechetical Directory, U.S.C.C. Publications, 1312 Massachusetts Ave., Washington, D.C. 20005, 1978.

Conversion Accounts

Griffin, Emilie, *Turning: Reflections on the Experience of Conversion*, Doubleday Image, 501 Franklin Ave., Garden City, NY 11530, 1982.

Merton, Thomas, *The Seven Storey Mountain*, Harcourt Brace Jovanovich, Publishers, San Diego, 1948.

Wallis, Jim, *The Call to Conversion*, Harper & Row, 1700 Montgomery St., San Francisco, CA 94111, 1982.

Adult Formation Materials

Burghardt, Walter J., S.J., *Seasons That Laugh and Weep*, Paulist Press, 997 Macarthur Blvd., Mahwah, NJ 07430, 1983.

DeBoy, James, *Getting Started in Adult Religious Education*, Paulist Press, 997 Macarthur Blvd., Mahwah, NJ 07430, 1979.

Hughes, Jane Wolford, ed. *Ministering to Adult Learners: A Skills Workbook for Christian Education Leaders*, USCC, 1312 Massachusetts Ave., NW, Washington, D.C. 20005, 1981.

Knowles, Malcolm, *The Modern Practice of Adult Education: Andragogy Versus Pedagogy*, Association Press, 291 Broadway, New York, NY 10007, 1975.

Parent, Neil, *Christian Adulthood: A Catechetical Resource 1982, 1983, 1984*, USCC, 1312 Massachusetts Ave., Washington D.C. 20005.

Schaefer, James R., *Program Planning for Adult Christian Education*, Paulist Press, 997 Macarthur Blvd., Mahwah, NJ 07430, 1972.

Sheehy, Gail, *Passages, Predictable Crises of Adult Life*, Bantam Books, Inc., 666 Fifth Ave., New York, NY 10019, 1976.

Westerhoff, John, *Will Our Children Have Faith?*, Seabury Press, 815 Second Avenue, New York, NY 10017, 1976.

Office for Church Life and Leadership, *The Church and Volunteers*, Church Leadership Resources, P.O. Box 179, St. Louis, MO 63166.

Others

Status of Implementation of the RCIA in the United States, Federation of Diocesan Liturgical Commissions.

Dyckman and Carroll, *Inviting the Mystic, Supporting the Prophet*, Paulist Press, 997 Macarthur Blvd., Mahwah, NJ 07430, 1981.

Huck, *A Triduum Sourcebook*, and *The Three Days*, Liturgy Training Publications, 155 East Superior Street, Chicago, IL 60611.

Cwack, *Annulments: Your Chance to Remarry in the Catholic Church*, Harper & Row, 1700 Montgomery St., San Francisco, CA 94111.

PLACES

Church buildings express the faith of the people who built them and that faith enriches our whole community. It can be a very good way to help catechumens experience the pluralism of the Catholic Church, and the changes it has experienced over its history.

Make use of your own parish church. The following sheets can be used with new members to maximize the value of your church building in your catechesis. Another way to use your building catechetically is to use the booklet "Welcome to Our Open House" (Paulist National Catholic Evangelization Association, 3031 4th Street NE, Washington, D.C. 20017). This explains the significance of the various elements in Catholic churches.

Visit neighboring parish churches, or churches of historical importance in your community.

The cathedral church should have special significance for catechumens, as well as all Catholics. Though tours or visits are helpful, this significance is clearest when catechumens gather at the cathedral with the bishop for the rite of election or the Chrism Mass, and experience its real meaning for them.

Church social service outreach centers should be known by catechumens, and, with them, the more organized opportunities for outreach. There is no better way to teach the essential nature of social justice than by seeing it in action and being part of it.

Using Your Parish Church: A Worksheet
Physically central to the life of the parish community of faith is the church building. Believing folk celebrate and commemorate life's greatest moments within its walls. These are the moments of birth, death, commitment, consecration, and forgiveness; the moments of sacrament.

Take a good look at your parish church building. What can it teach about life, faith, the Catholic faith? How can it be utilized to teach others? Get a pencil and paper and join me on a study tour.

What does your parish church look like when viewed from the street? What is the style of architecture, the main building material, the setting?

What makes your parish church special to you?

Is there a steeple, a bell tower, a baptistry, an identifying sign or cross, a cornerstone? Are there main doors, side doors?

What does the "view from the street" say about the faith family that worships within?

What is the floor plan, seating arrangement? Is this arrangement significant?

Do you know the name for the different sections of the building? The vestibule, sacristy, choir loft, etc. (circle those you know, add others.)

What furnishings are evident? Pews, altar table, pulpit, statues, sanctuary lamps, lecterns, presidential chair, etc. (circle those you know, add others.)

What statues are in your parish church? Whom do they represent? Where can you get more information about them?

What are the windows like? How can they be used to teach?

How do you feel when first entering your parish church? What is the mood?

Where is the baptismal font? Why? What does it look like?

Look at the confessionals, reconciliation room; what ideas about Penance do they reflect?

What does the layout of the sanctuary tell you about the Eucharistic life of the parish?

How is the Liturgy of the Word highlighted? The Liturgy of the Eucharist?

How do the people receive Communion?

What people have roles with the celebration of the Mass? (Priest, deacon, lector, commentator, server, other.) Have they distinguishing dress?

At weddings, what special things are done to highlight the uniqueness of this sacrament?

At funerals, what special things are done?

Are there any symbols within the parish building that show the parish community's unity with the bishop, the pope? Coat of arms, papal flag, etc.

(Worksheet prepared by Sr. Catherine Ann Birch, S.S.N.D., Coordinator of Teacher Learning Services, Division of Religious Education, Archdiocese of Baltimore.)

PEOPLE

People are a vital resource in the catechumenate. The RCIA specifically mentions sponsors, catechists, pastor. It also refers to the total community as primary initiating agent. Consider the people who might be special resources from your parish community.

Leaders of parish groups should welcome newcomers, and issue an invitation to participation in the groups they represent.

Old-timers, who have a deep sense of the history of the community, should be asked to share their wisdom as part of the total formation process.

Shut-ins who have experienced the Lord and the Church in sickness can be of great value in passing on the importance of community in the Lord. It is usually necessary that the catechumens go to the shut-in, since it is not possible for the shut-in to come to the catechumen. Such people can become prayer partners for the catechumens, continuing a spiritual relationship even when a physical one is not possible.

Young people with excitement at growing opportunities for responsibility for the Church should also be part of the formation of new members. Such contact is helpful both to the catechumen and to the young person who sees conversion face to face.

ARTS

The arts in your area may provide resources for you. Be aware of what is in museums, galleries, or special exhibits. Watch for religious centered performances like "Godspell", or "Mass"; plays with religious overtones like "Shadow Box", "Equus", "Agnes of God", may help us or hurt us, depending on how we react to them.

Television should also be in our range of interest. We must at least be aware of what is available, and react to it appropriately. Movies, popular music, and well-watched TV shows have great effects on our ministry. We must do our best to use them well.

There is a periodical with the specific goal of helping ministers use the arts in their work. It is called "Cultural Information Service", and is available through CIStems, Inc., P.O. Box 92, New York, NY 10156; edited by Rev. Frederick Brussat, it costs $25 per year.

AUDIO-VISUAL AIDS

Some suggestions for use with adults in the catechumenate process:

Harper Film Production
Pyramid Films
1536-14th Street
Box 1048
Santa Monica, CA 90496
"Covenant Promise" (15 minutes)
An overview of the history in the Old Testament, tracing themes of covenant, Messiah, prophecy, and judgement.

Ikonigraphics Inc.
P.O. Box 4454
Louisville, KY 40204
"History of the Church"
Series of 16 filmstrips, about ten minutes each, taking segments of Church history, from New Testament to post-Vatican II.

"Abraham", "David", "Ruth", "Joseph"
Old Testament filmstrip series, highlighting people from the Old Testament. Each strip is about 20 minutes in length.

Macmillan Films Inc.
34 MacQuesten Pkwy. S.
Mt. Vernon, NY 10550
"More" (5 minutes)

A humorous presentation of the real danger of consumerism.

Teleketics Films
Franciscan Communications
1229 S. Santee Street
Los Angeles, CA 90015
"Baptism, Sacrament of Belonging" (8 minutes)
The story of Alfredo, a young child who goes from being alone to having a family.

"Everyone, Everywhere" (11 minutes)
Mother Teresa's teaching that everyone, everywhere needs our love.

"Living Simply: Response to World Hunger"
Series of five filmstrips, pointing to some concrete ways we can do something about world hunger.

"Ruby Duncan, a Moving Spirit" (15 minutes)
Story of a black woman who changes things around her.

"The Widow's Mite" (20 minutes)
A story of conversion in the midst of poverty.

Video-cassette programs
Paulist National Catholic Evangelization Association
3031 4th Street NE
Washington, D.C. 20017
SHARE THE WORD video cassettes, VHS or Beta
Weekly teachings on the Sunday lectionary readings.

Paulist Press (material available for sale or rent)
997 Macarthur Blvd.
Mahwah, NJ 07430
201-825-7300
Search for Justice
Five-part video cassette series on Catholic social teaching and the American economy. (one hour each)

The Nuclear Dilemma
One two-hour video cassette divided into six segments, encourages informed discussion on the U.S. bishops' pastoral, "The Challenge of Peace"

Winter Rain
Six Images of Thomas Merton, written by Dr. Anthony Padovano, gifted author and Merton expert. (55 min.)

Julian
Julian of Norwich, a mystic of the 14th century, ap-

preciated the feminine aspects of God and lived with hope and joy though turmoil of her day. Her message is very much needed in our age of nuclear peril. (60 min.)

Some suggestions for use with RCIA and Evangelization teams
N.C.R. Cassettes
P.O. Box 281
Kansas City MO 64141
"Adult Initiation: Process and Ritual" (45 minutes)
Aiden Kavanagh

"Stages of Faith" (8 cassettes)
James Fowler

"The Radical Rite" (3 cassettes)
Tad Guzie

"Elements in Catechetical Formation" (42 minutes)
Nathan Mitchell

Paulist National Catholic Evangelization Association
3031 Fourth Street, NE
Washington, D.C. 20017
Four films (also 3/4 inch video cassettes) on Catholic evangelization in America today:
"What Is Catholic Evangelization Today"
"The Five Groups in America Most Enriched by Evangelization"
"Fifteen Basic Principles To Assist Catholic Lay Evangelizers"
"Contemporary Methods Used by Clergy and Laity To Evangelize"

SPECIAL GROUPS
To find resources for the deaf:
National Association of the Deaf (202-587-1788)
National Registry of Interpreters for the Deaf (202-588-2406)
International Catholic Deaf Association (202-588-4009)
same address for all three:
814 Thayer Avenue
Silver Spring, MD 20910

To find resources for the blind:
Xavier Society for the Blind
154 E. 23 Street
New York, NY 10010

Plough Publishing House
Society of Brothers
Norfolk CT 06058

Catholic Guild for the Blind
180 N. Michigan Avenue
Chicago, IL 60601

Division for Blind and Physically Handicapped
Library of Congress
Washington, D.C. 20542

American Bible Society
1865 Broadway
New York, NY 10163

When you meet mentally retarded adults wanting full membership

Mentally retarded adults should be as welcome to full initiation in the Church as other people. Most often, they are part of Catholic families who may have been put off long ago because of lack of understanding; or they may be persons being mainstreamed from institutions, looking for a community, and attracted by some concern they feel from our parishes.

Good preparation for them involves four aspects:

1. Membership in a peer group for spiritual sharing;

2. Experience of God's love, and a desire to be close to him in response;

3. Ability to distinguish Eucharist from regular bread;

4. Acceptance by the parish which would usually be shown during the major rites of the catechumenate.

Resources for the black community:
National Office of Black Catholics
1234 Massachusetts Ave. N.W.

Washington, D.C. 20005
202-635-1778

Josephite Pastoral Center
1200 Varnum Street N.E.
Washington, D.C. 20017
202-526-9270

What We Have Seen and Heard (Pastoral letter from the black bishops of the United States), St. Anthony Messenger Press, 1615 Republic Street, Cincinnati, OH 45210, 1984.
A study guide for this document is available through the Josephite Pastoral Center.

Resources for the Hispanic community:
Mexican American Cultural Center
3000 West French Place
San Antonio, TX 78228
512-732-2156

Secretariat for Hispanic Affairs
NCCB
1312 Massachusetts Ave., N.W.
Washington, D.C. 20005

Hispanic Presence: Challenge and Commitment (Bishops' statement), NCCB Publications Office, 1312 Massachusetts Avenue N.W., Washington, D.C. 20005, 202-659-6835.

Hispanic Resources for Evangelization Catechesis, Cecilia J. Morales, Jr., Ed., 1981, NCCB Committee on Evangelization; in Spanish; $4.00

Sicilia, "Adapting RCIA and the Hispanic Parish", C.I.R. III, Catechumenate H.